Serving Teens
through
Readers' Advisory

ALA Readers' Advisory Series

The Horror Readers' Advisory:
The Librarian's Guide to Vampires,
Killer Tomatoes, and Haunted Houses

The Science Fiction and Fantasy Readers' Advisory:
The Librarian's Guide to Cyborgs, Aliens, and Sorcerers

The Mystery Readers' Advisory:
The Librarian's Clues to Murder and Mayhem

The Readers' Advisory Guide to Genre Fiction

The Romance Readers' Advisory:
The Librarian's Guide to Love in the Stacks

The Short Story Readers' Advisory:
A Guide to the Best

Heather Booth

Serving Teens
through
Readers' Advisory

American Library Association
Chicago   2007

Composition by ALA Editions in Janson Text and Helvetica Condensed using InDesign CS2.

Printed on 50-pound white offset, a pH-neutral stock, and bound in 10-point coated cover stock by Victor Graphics.

The paper used in this publication meets the minimum requirements of American National Standard for Information Sciences—Permanence of Paper for Printed Library Materials, ANSI Z39.48-1992. ∞

Library of Congress Cataloging-in-Publication Data
Booth, Heather, 1978–
    Serving teens through readers' advisory / Heather Booth.
      p.   cm. — (ALA readers' advisory series)
    Includes bibliographical references and index.
    ISBN 0-8389-0930-2 (alk. paper)
    1. Readers' advisory services—United States. 2. Libraries and teenagers—United States. 3. Teenagers—Books and reading—United States. 4. Young adult literature—Bibliography. I. Title.
    Z711.55.B66 2007
    028.5—dc22   2006036134

ISBN-10: 0-8389-0930-2
ISBN-13: 978-0-8389-0930-0

Printed in the United States of America

11 10 09 08 07   5 4 3 2 1

To my parents, Gayle and James Booth, my first and best teachers, and to Paul

Contents

Figures

● ● ● ● ● ● ● ● ● ● ● ● ● ● ● ●

Preface

● ● ● ● ● ● ● ● ● ● ● ● ● ●

Most readers have a story about the book that changed their lives—the book that turned them on to the power of books and pleasure of reading. This experience often seems to happen during adolescence, and for good reasons. Teenagers are undergoing a sea change in their physical, emotional, intellectual, and social selves. Books, with the information and stories contained within, can serve as companions, guides, and mirrors in this complex, unsettling, and exciting stage of life. If you probe a little deeper into the stories of these landmark books of adolescence and ask how people came upon their books, there are often stories about the friend who passed a favored paperback on to them, the relative who engaged them in a conversation about what they had read, or even the librarian who suggested the book in the first place.

This book is intended to assist librarians and others who work with teens and books in making more book connections that teenage patrons will remember many years from now, as well as in making connections that provide reading experiences that are highly enjoyed but might be easily forgotten. It will not tell you exactly which book to give to which teen patron, nor is it an all-in-one comprehensive guidebook for a general readers' advisory or young adult services department. Many other resources discussed in this book are excellent sources for that type of information. Rather, this book works to explain why young adults need and want high-quality reading experiences and functions as a guide for those interested in providing teen readers with this crucial and enjoyable service.

In part 1, we briefly explore the long relationship that libraries have had with teens and how this history affects the present situation in which we are functioning. Then the theoretical underpinnings of the work of readers' advisory for teens will be introduced as we investigate the research describing why and how recreational reading is beneficial for teens.

Part 2 provides the basic foundations on which to build a readers' advisory service for teens. In this section, library generalists or those new to readers' advisory and young adult literature will gain introductions to those fields and tips on how to become more fluent in them.

Part 3 walks the reader through a typical readers' advisory interaction with a teen patron, offering concrete suggestions on how to discuss books and specific questions to ask in order to make the best match possible between a teen and a book.

With any age or interest group come special situations. Teens and the special circumstances that occur in working with their reading needs are discussed in part 4, including homework assignments and helping caregivers select books for the teens in their lives.

Finally, part 5 will guide the librarian to sources that will help make the connection between teens and specific books and will provide guidance and ideas for branching out from simple face-to-face interactions and leading a department in more successful readers' advisory for young adults.

Overall, this book should serve as the beginning of a journey to provide high-quality readers' advisory service to the young adults in our communities. Of course, there are always more books to read and teens with whom to share them. I encourage readers, in addition to reading and putting into practice the information and suggestions here, to reach out to the teens in your libraries, schools, and lives to listen to their concerns, interests, and motivations relating to books, reading, and life. Although you may deeply desire to be the librarian who passes on incredible reading experiences, being the librarian who listens to teens' interests with respect and empathy will almost always lead to capturing the essence of teen readers' advisory.

Acknowledgments

● ● ● ● ● ● ● ● ● ● ● ● ● ● ●

My sincerest thanks to all who helped me, encouraged me, and listened to me throughout the process of writing this book. I have been so fortunate to work at the Downers Grove Public Library, an environment that encourages and endorses high-quality readers' advisory service for all ages under the guidance of our director, Christopher Bowen. Joyce Saricks hired me into an amazingly supportive department, introduced me to the possibilities in writing about library service, and insisted that I was indeed capable of writing this book. My supervisor, Sue O'Brien, and my coworkers in the outstanding Readers' Advisory and Audio Department, Debbie Deady, Sheila Guenzer, Nana Oakey-Campana, Nicole Suarez, Marianne Trautvetter, and Terri Williams, taught me how to be an effective readers' advisor and generously shared their friendship and many years of experience with me.

Many people read and offered comments and suggestions on various parts of this book, especially Gayle Booth, who read every word. Michael Cox, Kelly Czarnecki, Abby Koehler, Jessica Moyer, Sue O'Brien, Joyce Saricks, and Paul Zaremba read and reacted to the ideas and chapters in progress. I especially thank Jessica Moyer, Terri Williams, Michael Cox, and Kelly Czarnecki for their suggestions about the popular authors lists.

Joyce Saricks, Georgine Olson, and Neal Wyatt generously shared elements of their own writing. I thank them for these excellent examples and instructional tools in the field of readers' advisory. My editor at ALA Editions, Laura Pelehach, encouraged me throughout the writing process.

I wish to acknowledge and thank the teenagers in the Downers Grove Public Library's Teen Advisory Board who let me into their conversation circles about books. They allowed me to ask them questions and offer suggestions, and in turn, I have grown from the questions they have asked and the suggestions they have offered me.

Finally, I must acknowledge the love and support of my husband, Paul, who shared the entirety of our engagement and first year of marriage with the planning and writing of this book and has always encouraged me to be . . . ambitious.

Thank you.

Part One

● ● ● ● ● ● ● ● ● ● ● ● ● ● ●

What Do We Do and Why Do We Do It?

1 ● A Brief History of Teens and Reading in Libraries

How have libraries served teens' reading needs and interests in the past? Before delving into how and why to shape a read-ers' advisory service for teens, let us look at the evolution of teen services in the United States.

Librarianship and the publishing industry have made great strides in service to young adults—first in acknowledging that services and products specific to the age range are necessary, and second in examining how to extend these services and products. When thinking about and participating in a readers' advisory service for young adults, it is helpful to keep in mind that the issues we face with regard to teens and reading are not new. There has always been a concern that adolescents are not reading enough, or that they are not reading the right things, or even that they will be "damaged" if they read the wrong things. That said, there have always been innovators and youth advocates in the field concerned with and working toward provid-ing youth with reading material not just for enrichment and refinement but also for pleasure and enjoyment. Though the approaches taken with regard to teenagers varied throughout the past century, there has been a general progression toward a more cooperative relationship in which librarians work with teens to serve their reading and information needs, and away from the moralistic or instructive roles of the early 1900s.

Samuel Swett Green, a Worcester, Massachusetts, librarian and later president of the American Library Association (ALA), commented on work-ing with young people in a much-quoted article in an 1876 issue of *Library Journal*.[1] He said, "There are few pleasures comparable to that of associating continually with curious and vigorous young minds, and of aiding them in realizing their ideals."[2] Even at that early date, near the inception of American librarianship as we know it today, aiding youth in attaining their ideals was an acknowledged goal, task, and pleasure. The reality of service to adolescents, though, reflects a less-than-open perspective on what these "vigorous young

1

minds" should be reading. In the nineteenth century and early part of the twentieth century, library service to youth was different from its equivalent today. The main reason was that teenagers were different. Psychologists first discussed adolescence as a period of life distinct from childhood and adulthood in 1904.[3] The Fair Labor Standards Act, which regulated the age of workers, did not take effect until 1938, before which time many teenagers were working long hours for wages rather than attending school for their own betterment. Many working teens found vocational training materials, instructional books, and assistance in using them at libraries. The other significant type of material offered to adolescents—in or out of the workforce—was classic literature intended to improve their "taste," motivated by fear that lesser texts would be harmful to a child's intellectual development.[4] It was in the 1920s and 1930s that public libraries began devoting services to youth and the needs befitting their age.[5]

As time progressed and more adolescents remained in school through their teen years, educators and libraries had to acknowledge that a one-book-fits-all method for reading suggestion was not adequate. Amid the growing and changing population in the schools, the 1920s saw a growing conflict between the classics and popular fiction, with young people, not surprisingly, expressing a preference for the popular and educators remaining concerned with providing a well-rounded reading experience.[6]

In the 1930s and 1940s a movement arose to address the issue on a larger scale. The Board on Library Service to Children and Young People in School and Public Libraries was formed at ALA in 1932, and the first professional text specifically about teens and reading, *The Public Library and the Adolescent*, by E. Leyland, was published in 1937.[7] Librarians began examining why the teens they worked with might be hesitant to read. They found that a lack of material adolescents connected with, being pressed to read books of "value" rather than those of interest, and limited reading ability topped the list of concerns. The impact of required reading began to be examined, and many librarians led a shift toward encouraging more imaginative, adventurous, or romantic reading as a way to expand young people's horizons and experience.[8]

The postwar years brought a flurry of changes for groups dedicated to improving library services for youth, leading to many articles in professional publications advising librarians on how to best serve young people. Honors were created both for books for teens to read and for librarians serving teens. The Association of Young People's Librarians (AYPL) of ALA prepared its first list titled "Significant Adult Books for Teens and Interesting Books," which in 1952 became "Best Books for Young Adults."[9] In 1954, the Grolier Award (now the Scholastic Library Publishing Award) began honoring librarians who made an "unusual contribution to the stimulation and guidance of reading by children and young people." Its fourth recipient, Margaret A. Edwards (1957), was the first librarian to be honored specifically for striving to serve teenagers.[10] In the years since, the Grolier Award has acknowledged many more librarians in service to young adults. New publications aimed toward teenage readers flourished as well, partly in response to the idea that such books would help teens adjust to the realities of young life in the face of war, but also simply because there was a market for them. "Not only did the adolescent subculture develop following the second world war, but it was a time of affluence, and money was available for such luxury items as books for young people of a narrow age range," concluded Margaret Hutchinson, in an expression of the ongoing connection between teens, their finances, popular culture, and the publishing industry.[11]

In 1957, the first wave of the baby boom generation was nearing adolescence and the Young Adult Services Division of the American Library Association split from the Children's Library Association, forming what is today the Young Adult Library Services Association (YALSA). With more teen novels, comics, and popular materials and more youth services departments in libraries to serve teens, librarians continued to note how the availability of material affects teen reading habits. The propensity of teens to be drawn to topics of interest, not just format, marketing, or skill level, was noted in 1958:

> Evidence is reasonably good that they like or dislike a book or a poem or a biography or a play pretty much on the basis of its subject matter. Surprisingly, the so-called difficult books are not difficult if the subject matter is appealing, and books that are called easy books are not easy for the adolescent if the subject matter does not fall within these established boundaries.[12]

Yet some people continued to advocate leading teens to more complex or classic titles rather than simply helping teens enjoy books of their own choosing. This persisted into the 1960s, when publishing in the field of library services for young adults once again increased, most notably with Margaret A. Edward's groundbreaking and classic 1969 work on the topic, *The Fair Garden and the Swarm of Beasts*.[13]

The 1970s were an exciting time for teens and libraries. Edwards's book armed librarians with a practical tool with which to build library service to young adults. An array of new books by S. E. Hinton, Paul Zindel, Robert Cormier, and others launched the first golden age of young adult literature. And the largest generation of children the country had ever seen were reaching their teens. Librarians who served teens were off and running. National standards of practice were developed as youth issues worked their way into important foundation documents such as the "Free Access to Minors" interpretation of the Library Bill of Rights in 1972 and YASD's "Directions for Library Service to Young Adults" in 1977. Journals specifically for those who work with teens like the *Young Adult Alternative Newsletter* (1972), *School Library Journal* (1974), and *Voice of Youth Advocates* (1978) were founded.[14] Also at this point in time, enough had occurred in the field of library service to teens to merit reflection. The first "Best of the Best" selection of books for teens was produced in 1975, highlighting the best books from the past fifteen years.

The teen paperback romance boom hit in the 1980s, and for the first time a teen novel, a Sweet Valley High series super edition, made it onto the *New York Times* paperback best-seller list.[15] Many strong YA authors who are still writing today, such as Lawrence Yep, M. E. Kerr, Chris Crutcher, Jane Yolen, and Cynthia Voigt, emerged as forces in the genre. Additionally, multicultural literature began to flourish and gain interest. The progress of professional organizations in supporting and enriching library service to teens continued to broaden and generated more and more programs and materials. In 1981, the guidelines "Young Adults Deserve the Best" were developed to outline the skills and competencies needed to effectively serve youth in libraries. Interest in the topic of teens and books was no longer limited to concerned educators and librarians; it spread to the popular media, and powerful interest groups latched on to it.

The 1990s ushered in a new era of progress in the profession. Library services to teens focused on inclusiveness and collaborating with teens to create good teen spaces and collections. With more and more high-quality and highly appealing YA literature being written every day, librarians were better able to address the diverse needs and interests of teen readers. In 1993, the Excellence in Library Services to Young Adults project was begun. Funded by the Margaret A. Edwards Trust, the project has succeeded in honoring and publicizing innovative efforts by libraries across the country.[16] The fourth edition of the book featuring these exceptional projects was published in 2004.[17]

Book awards specifically focused on teen literature, the Printz and the Alex Awards, were created. Teen Read Week was set aside in October of each year to encourage and promote teen reading and involvement with libraries.[18] A focus on designing spaces that were geared to the specific needs and interests of teen patrons emerged, and in 1994 the Los Angeles Public Library created its innovative Teen'Scape, the first space of its kind in a public library.[19] The work of a young adult librarian had changed enough that the guidelines for youth librarians created in 1981, "Young Adults Deserve the

Best," were revised and updated in 1998. The number of new publications in the field increased once again, this time focusing on practical applications of reading and library theory and of the knowledge gained over many years. Among these were the first editions of *Connecting Young Adults and Libraries* and *Bare Bones: Young Adult Services; Tips for Public Library Generalists.*[20]

Two momentous things happened in the world of teens and reading during the late 1990s. The Internet was one, Harry Potter was the other, and the full implications of both are yet to be known. The Internet gave teens much more immediate access to information—including information about books—than they had ever had before. Harry made reading accessible and cool for many teens who may not have given books or libraries a second glance. Interestingly, the Internet and J. K. Rowling's fantasy series set in a British boarding school have had similar effects on library service to teens. Both have raised concerns about content and censorship, both continue to influence spin-off titles and technologies that librarians must sometimes run to keep up with, and, most important of all, both have given teens a reason to come to the library.

Given two cultural phenomena that directly and positively affected library service, librarians in the early 2000s rose to the occasion. Libraries are now examining their role in the lives of young people in a more holistic manner, with many programs using the Search Institute's "40 Developmental Assets for Adolescent Development" to understand the *why* behind the impact of library services and to build programs and fill roles that help teens grow into positive and productive adults.[21] We are supported now by the Young Adult Library Services Association (YALSA), which, at this writing, is the fastest growing division of the American Library Association.[22]

The reigning philosophy of young adult services has become "Work *with* teens, not *for* them," and programs and services are reflecting this ideal. Teen Read Week now includes open online voting for the Teen's Top Ten booklist. All books on the ballot are selected by teens from school and public library groups across the country who read, discuss the merits of their favorite titles, and nominate what they feel are the best books published for their age group over the past year. Teen reviews are now a common find on library websites, and you, dear reader, have a book in your hand to help you continue the progress of teens and librarians working with one another.

With the dawn of the new millennium, librarians are much changed yet very much the same as those who laid the groundwork for serving teens and connecting them with books over one hundred years ago. Like our forebears, we continue to grapple with issues such as what is the right material to hand to young people and what is the correct role of libraries in the lives of teens. Now, though, in addition, we wonder how to present and if and how we should collect graphic novels, pop-culture nonfiction, edgy novels, or teen-authored works. Most libraries have a teen space, however limited, but the question may be whether or not it is staffed with someone who identifies as a young adult librarian or has the training and interest in working with this age group. We may know of the most engaging and inspiring books for young adults, but do we know how to talk about them in a way that effectively conveys their appeal to our teenage patrons?

This work intends to extend the tradition of progress and continuing education for librarians in service to teenagers. It will serve as a guide to the practical aspects of readers' advisory work with teens, explore the philosophies and rationale underlying such work for libraries, and examine the crucial role of readers' advisory in the development of our teen patrons. Almost anyone who works at a public service desk in a library will need to do readers' advisory work with teens at some time or another. Whether you are already an experienced readers' advisor for adults who wishes to expand your skills into a new demographic, a library student who has yet to embark on the exciting work that lies ahead, or a library generalist who is readying to add a new skill, this work will lay out the playing field, point out a few key moves, and, I hope, be the pep talk you need to get through the tough plays.

Notes

1. Then *American Library Journal*.

2. Samuel Swett Green, "Personal Relations between Librarian and Readers," *American Library Journal* 1 (1876): 74–81.

3. Michael Cart, *From Romance to Realism: 50 Years of Growth and Change in Young Adult Literature* (New York: HarperCollins, 1996), 4.

4. Margaret Hutchinson, "Fifty Years of Young Adult Reading, 1921–1971," in *Young Adult Literature in the Seventies: A Selection of Readings* (Metuchen, NJ: Scarecrow Press, 1978), 40.

5. Anthony Bernier, Mary K. Chelton, Christine A. Jenkins, and Jennifer Burek Pierce, comps., "Two Hundred Years of Young Adult Library Services History," e-VOYA web-only article, full-length web version (June 2005), http://www.voya.com/whatsinvoya/web_only_articles/Chronology_200506.shtml.

6. Hutchinson, "Fifty Years of Young Adult Reading," 40–42.

7. Bernier et al., "Two Hundred Years of Young Adult Library Services History."

8. Hutchinson, "Fifty Years of Young Adult Reading," 43–45.

9. Carol Starr, "A Brief History of the Young Adult Services Division," *Young Adult Library Services Association Handbook*, http://www.ala.org/ala/yalsa/aboutyalsa/briefhistory.htm.

10. "Scholastic Library Publishing Recipients (Formerly Grolier Award)," American Library Association website, http://www.ala.org/ala/awardsbucket/scholastic/scholasticawardrecipients.htm.

11. Hutchinson, "Fifty Years of Young Adult Reading," 47.

12. Ibid., 51.

13. Margaret A. Edwards, *The Fair Garden and the Swarm of Beasts* (New York: Hawthorne Books, 1969).

14. Bernier et al., "Two Hundred Years of Young Adult Library Services History."

15. Cart, *From Romance to Realism*, 105.

16. Bernier et al., "Two Hundred Years of Young Adult Library Services History."

17. Renée Vaillancourt McGrath, ed., *Excellence in Library Services to Young Adults*, 4th ed. (Chicago: ALA Editions, 2004).

18. The Printz Award committee was formed in 1999, and the first awards were presented in 2000. "Michael Printz Award Committee Description," YALSA website, http://www.ala .org/ala/yalsa/aboutyalsab/michaellprintz.htm. The Alex Award was established in 1997, the first awards were presented in 1998, and it became an official ALA award in 2001. "Alex Award Committee Description," YALSA website, http://www.ala.org/ala/yalsa/ aboutyalsab/alexcommittee.htm. Teen Read Week was established in 1998, http://www .ala.org/ala/yalsa/teenreading/teenreading.htm.

19. Bernier et al., "Two Hundred Years of Young Adult Library Services History."

20. Patrick Jones, *Connecting Young Adults and Libraries* (New York: Neal-Schuman, 1992); Mary K. Chelton, *Bare Bones: Young Adult Services; Tips for Public Library Generalists* (Chicago: ALA Editions, 1993).

21. Search Institute, http://www.search-institute.org.

22. Pam Spencer Holley, "President's Message: Fall YALS," YALSA website, http://www.ala .org/ala/yalsa/fall.htm.

2.

Why Teens Need to Read, Why They Want to Read

Understanding the motivations of teens who read for pleasure is crucial to laying the foundation for the why of readers' advisory for teens, upon which the how is placed. In this chapter, we will look at the research and anecdotal evidence about the benefits of recreational and informational teen reading as well as explore how recreational reading and forming a relationship with the library contribute to the overall success of young people. This is the chapter to revisit when you are sure that you cannot read another teen problem novel, when you are frustrated by your library's lack of funds for collecting teen materials, or when you have a particularly active bunch of teens in the library who do not appear to want anything to do with the books. Reading is important to teens. It is important for their educational prospects, their personal enrichment, and their pure enjoyment. Teens who read are important to our local community and to our greater world community. *This* is why we do what we do.

This chapter will cover

- What motivates teens to read
- The benefits teens gain from reading
- Why teen reading is important to the community

Why Is Recreational Reading Important?

It Improves Students' Education

It has been well established that children and teens who read frequently have a more developed vocabulary, are better spellers, and have a better understanding of grammar than those who do not read. Compared to spoken language, written language tends to have a higher frequency of complex, uncommon words. Studies have shown that the vocabulary of those students who read frequently after the fifth grade benefits even more from reading than before fifth grade.[1] Contrary to the idea of "good books" being more educational and useful to the academic success of teens than "fluff," it appears that the nature of written language itself will help increase vocabulary, irrespective of the work's literary complexity. In *The Power of Reading*, Stephen Krashen compiles strong evidence indicating that it is not spelling instruction that leads to good spellers, it is free, voluntary reading.[2] Research also indicates that students and adults who are identified as creative, as good thinkers, or as exhibiting a higher level of cultural literacy are those who also read more.[3]

Several researchers have discovered the academic benefits of self-selected recreational reading. When teens voluntarily read about topics of interest to them, their attitudes about reading improve and they make a greater effort to read nonrecreational or assigned reading. Even reading material that appears very simplistic or nonacademic will increase the confidence of students and "encourage them to tackle more technical reading materials in school."[4] Jim Trelease introduced the idea of a home run book, a book that sparks an initial interest in reading. Research done by Joanne Ujiie and Krashen, based on Trelease's concept, suggests that just one positive book-reading experience can lead to lifelong enjoyment of reading and, by extension, all of its inherent benefits.[5] Graphic novels or comics, newspapers, magazines, "fluff" or "trashy" novels, audiobooks, and topics of interest on the Internet are frequently dismissed as not "real" reading materials. But in fact, for many teens, these are significant forms of reading from which they gain information, visual literacy skills, vocabulary, and more. Again, it is the process of reading written language that benefits vocabulary and language acquisition—not the perceived quality of the package. This "light" reading is actually very beneficial because it is effortless reading. It is this effortless (or less strenuous) reading that improves reading fluency, which in turn improves the reading confidence of students and often leads to more advanced or complex reading choices.

It Provides Intangible Benefits outside of School

It is rarely questioned that reading benefits the educational lives of teens and improves their scholastic performance. The issue that readers' advisors for teens must defend more frequently is the less quantifiable value that recreational reading has in the lives of teens outside of the educational setting. Is it just a nice hobby, a safe and low-cost activity, or something much more? It is all of these. Students typically do unassigned reading for three important reasons: to gain information, to escape, or to gain an affirming connection. These reasons are not mutually exclusive. They often work in combination, they are equally important in their own time and place, and they each play a role in feeding the needs of teens in the nonscholastic realms of their lives. Let us look at some examples of how these reading motivations play out in the lives of teens.

The Role of Magazines

As mentioned above, teen magazine reading is an important element of recreational reading. Magazines that address topical interests such as gaming, music, animals, sports, anime, or specific hobbies (model aircraft, photography, knitting) are a popular form of recreational reading and provide teens with information. By virtue of their very existence, topical magazines also convey the message that a topic that interests one teen is also of interest to others. Topical magazine reading can also be a great escape. For example, *Mad* magazine, *National Geographic Adventure*, and *US Weekly* can and do provide a mini vacation in a world of humor, fame, or international exploration, giving teens a break from the world they live in every day as well as exposing them to opportunities and ideas beyond those close to home.

Teen fashion magazines—like many of their adult counterparts—are filled with material that teen girls crave and read to confirm that they are OK and not alone. Some adults question the emotional and social benefits of articles on dieting, dating advice, and pop stars. But the reality is that especially for younger teen girls first experiencing the physical changes of puberty and the emotional adjustments of starting new schools, realigning their social groups, and seeking involvement in romantic relationships, magazines such as *Seventeen, CosmoGIRL!* and *Teen People* function as manuals for how to get through the teenage years.[6] Unfortunately missing from the teen print magazine market are publications that could provide the best of the teen glossy magazines (stories of real teens who have overcome adversity) and the pop culture savvy to keep the appeal up (fashion and makeup tips, celebrity tie-ins) and still convey the information in a way that preserves and improves the self-image and confidence of girls in this vulnerable age, instead of constantly extolling the virtues of dieting and the ever-present quest for the perfect prom date. *Sassy* magazine of the early nineties, before its Peterson's buyout in 1994, is sorely missed on this count.[7] Regardless of the content, teen magazines are a hugely popular source of reading material, second to books and far above the next reported choice of reading material, according to a recent SmartGirl.org survey in conjunction with YALSA's Teen Read Week.[8] Any library serving teens should keep this in mind and do its best to carve out space in the budget and on the shelves for magazines with appeal for local teens.

Three Novel Examples

Reading to gain information can happen intentionally or by chance. Teens may seek out instructional books on skateboarding tricks or knitting to further their interests. Or they may pick up a novel and find that they are getting much more out of it than an entertaining story. The phenomenon of Dan Brown's *The Da Vinci Code* has crossed over into the teen arena and is a great example of the blend of escapist and informational reading that teens encounter. Recently, a teen approached the desk looking for something to read after *The Da Vinci Code*. In the course of the readers' advisory interview, he brought up that initially he just enjoyed the fast pace, the romantic action, and the mystery element. After a pause, he said, "You know, I learned a lot too." Despite the controversy surrounding the veracity of many of Brown's assertions, the novel does contain lots of interesting information about art history and the life of Leonardo Da Vinci, and in this case, it sparked the teen's curiosity about some great religious mysteries. After finding a few more fast-paced thrillers to read, he sought a nonfiction work on Jesus as a historical figure.

An avid reader in our teen advisory group is a great fan of fantasy books. She is a senior in high school, involved in activities and her community, academically successful, and a dedicated advocate and lover of animals of all kinds. Recently, she picked up 'Asta Bowen's *Wolf: The Journey Home*, which is told entirely through the eyes of a wolf that had been captured and reintroduced into the wilds of Montana. Initially, she was drawn to the book because the main character was a wolf and she was interested in learning about animal life. She later articulated why stories about wizards, knights, fantastical places, animals, and this book in particular are appealing to her.

> It's unique to have a book focus on animals the way that *Wolf* does, without being the biography of a pet or a furry fantasy such as Brian Jacques's Redwall series (though I am a fan of both). Not all teen books have to be about teens—in fact, I am often turned off by those books. I live the life of a teenager; I do not need to read about it, too!

How much more of an escape can there be than to read about life from the perspective of a different species?

Some teens may choose escapist reading that contains idealized romantic elements, details of life in moneyed society as depicted in the television series *The OC*, or rough-edged accounts of teens on the street that they can contrast with their own personal experiences. Or, like the teen in our advisory group, they may choose to read about animals and faraway places. The type of escapist reading that teens choose may vary, but the end result is the same. From time to time, we all need a break from our everyday world, and turning to fiction to fill that need is an easy, inexpensive, and safe way to indulge our fantasies—regardless of whether the alternative world is around the corner, around the world, or on the other side of the galaxy.

One of my favorite quotes about reading comes from C. S. Lewis, who said, "We read to know we are not alone." As much as the teen years are about socializing, they can also be a lonely time as young people branch out and away from their families, seek a more individual identity, and reach out to friends and social groups. Recreational reading feeds a very real need for connection—even if the connection is with fictional characters. A sophomore in our library's teen advisory board recently read Louisa May Alcott's *Little Women* for the first time. She commented that she "was amazed at how realistic the girls were" and noted in a review of the book, "Though we watch the girls transform from little women to mothers, one thing never changes—a family will always be there for you in good times and bad." This teen chose to read *Little Women* herself, and in the midst of her modern adolescence, she found a very affirming connection with the March sisters from a distant time.

What the Internet Reveals about Teens and Recreational Reading

Reading for connection may happen much more deliberately than in the case of the teen who found affirmation in *Little Women*. Teens may seek out a character they can relate to who has dealt with a similar difficult issue, such as rape, divorce, loss of a loved one, sexual pressures, drug use, or discrimination. Given the sensitive nature of these topics, readers' advisory requests are more likely to come from parents or teachers than from the teens themselves, unless the teen and the librarian have already established a relationship. Reaching out in a time of emotional need is difficult for anyone to do, and teens may be hesitant to approach a librarian to ask for an appropriate reading suggestion. Nonetheless, some teens do seek out such assistance. A look at online message boards where teens discuss books can reveal how reading helps teens feel connected and affirmed, with many suggestions for reading traded back and forth among the participants. These discussions pop up in a variety of places: personal blogs, publishers' websites, online journals of writers themselves, sites designed for the sole purpose of discussing books, and even online networking communities like MySpace.com.

Regarding David Levitan's lighthearted love story *Boy Meets Boy*, set in an idealized town where differences in sexual orientation and variations in gender identity are celebrated and accepted, a teen posted,

> I just finished the book yesterday and i loved it! I am a gay teenager and it appealed to me in so many ways. *I just wish i knew as many gay people as Paul does—i don't know any.* But I reccomend [*sic*] it to anyone! I seriously hope for a sequel!! [emphasis added][9]

Not only did the novel provide a character that the reader could relate to and a bit of escapism in the form of a town where being gay is no different from having brown hair, but it also gave the reader a connection he desires and lacks in his own life. Occasionally, interest groups will accuse libraries of being unnecessarily full of "gay books," but comments like the one above illustrate the important role that fiction featuring homosexual characters plays in libraries. These books affirm to gay teens that they are not alone—that there are others out there to whom they can relate. In the same way, teens who are adopted, those with disabilities, those in unhappy relationships, city dwellers, country dwellers, athletes, and musicians all can find books about relatable characters when they visit the library.

On TeenInc.com, the web presence of the print journal and book series featuring the writing, reviewing, and art of teens nationwide, a review of the first book in Ann Brashares's blockbuster series The Sisterhood of the Traveling Pants reads,

> A major story line tells how one member, Tibby, goes through an extremely emotional time with the death of someone close to her. This section will make you cry, laugh, and smile. You will travel the journey with her and all the girls in the sisterhood. I really enjoyed this book. It is great for girls dealing with similar issues.[10]

Because it features four friends, separated for the first time over summer vacation, Brashares's novel gives readers a wonderful reading experience—escapism in some story lines and something to relate to in others. And because just about any girl could relate to at least one of the issues among the four friends, it is a sure bet when suggesting books to a teen who may be reluctant to discuss her reading preferences. (Sure bets will be discussed further in chapter 11.)

Sometimes a book goes beyond simply providing a likable character to whom a teen can relate. Sometimes the connection is profound and truly life affirming. A particularly poignant entry from the virtual guest book on Sarah Dessen's homepage (*Truth about Forever, Dreamland*) illustrates quite eloquently the type of connection that teens may gain through recreational reading. "Dear Sarah," the teen writes,

I have just finished reading, The Truth about Forever.

I loved it!

I have read other books by you (That Summer, Someone Like You, This Lullaby) but The Truth about Forever is my favorite. I could really relate to it.

My sister died last spring and my whole world seemed to change. No one was prepared for it. It just happened. Like Macy I was quiet about the subject. I barely even cried at the funeral. But my heart feels broken.

I don't talk to my parents about the way I feel. It's too hard and in some way I feel I have to be the strong one. Sometimes though, out of no where, tears will come and I have that sudden urge to find my parents and just talk to them about my sister. But the tears leave just as quickly as they come and I'm back to whatever I'm doing: homework, reading, watching TV. I never go to my parents.

But reading this book comforted me. I know Macy is just a fictional character, but in a way I feel that she is real. That she's my character.

Macy talked to her mom; she realized it was OK to be sad. Someday, I hope I can talk to my parents—I'll take it one step at a time—and I know now it's OK to be sad. In this book you say there is no such thing as perfect, but the way you described Macy's feelings, what she does and doesn't want to do . . . well, it was as close to perfect as you can get.

Thank you so much for writing this novel. You've given me hope.[11]

"You've given me hope." A book—a novel—has given hope to a teen who felt alone and incapable of dealing with the feelings that were engulfing her. What better outcome could we hope for? A single book had the power to help a young woman deal with her sadness over a tragic loss and understand that life must go on. *This* is why we do what we do. *This* is the true and best benefit of readers' advisory for recreational teen reading.

Self-Selected Reading, Trying on Adulthood, and Safe Risk-Taking

When teens self-select recreational reading, they choose for themselves what and when they want to read. This autonomy is something that adults enjoy and never question. But for teens and even younger children, it is an important stepping-stone that empowers them and their choices. Reading allows teens to explore ideas, scenarios, and attitudes with which they may or may not agree or identify. This exploration allows teens to dip their toes into the larger world around them and clarify their sense of self and personal stance on various issues. While reading, teens are trying on attitudes and ideas for the future.

Many schools, libraries, and communities are working with the principles put forth by the Search Institute, an organization whose goal is to create healthy youth and communities. Key to the institute's mission are its "40 Developmental Assets" for youth in various stages of their lives. These forty assets are "positive experiences and personal qualities that young people need to grow up healthy, caring, and responsible," and not surprisingly, one of the assets for adolescents is reading for pleasure.[12] Within the institute's framework, reading is an important indicator of a commitment to lifelong learning. The connection between reading for pleasure and future academic success, as discussed in the first section of this chapter, is proven by the Search Institute's research. But reading for pleasure helps teens develop in other realms of their lives as well.

Margaret Mackey elaborates on this issue in her impressive analysis of why young people choose to read books and why they should be allowed to continue to do so.[13] In an indictment of structured reading programs such as Accelerated Reader and the inclination that many adults have to discourage lower-level reading material or direct young people to specific types of books, Mackey says:

> Too many adults want children to read, and read with enthusiasm, without conceding to them any vestige of the sense of real control that is one of the social and psychological triumphs of reading. Children, who are trying to "win at growing up," as Beverly Cleary's Ramona so succinctly expresses the challenge, are being given a false passport that lets them only into a fenced-off field.[14]

She likens reading to walking: if children were told when, how fast, with what style, and where they were allowed to walk, what would the joy be in stretching their legs? Young people must be allowed and encouraged to seek out self-selected recreational reading because reading is a developmental skill that can take them far, but only if they are allowed to discover its potential.

Additionally, Mackey discusses the importance of risk taking in the reading choices of youth, pointing out how many of the most popular materials challenge societal norms or accepted standards of behavior with a "clever wickedness." *Mad* magazine is a prime example of this—critically acclaimed material is satirized and mocked with a devious wink at the reader.

Concerned adults fret over young people's perceived lack of interest in reading, predicting all kinds of dire intellectual and social outcomes as society is "dumbed down" and kids blank out over video games and stupid television rather than honing their wits on reading. Yet much of the well-meaning advice concerning young people and their reading takes no account of (or perversely blocks from consideration) the idea that young people are looking for moral and aesthetic challenges, preferably real ones that involve some genuine imaginative risk.

If teens are not finding this imaginative risk in their reading material, there is no lack of it in popular TV, movie, Internet, or video game culture. Reading may not replace the risk taking teens choose to experience by playing violent video games, exploring different religious beliefs on the Internet, or watching sexy escapades on television. But if they are exposed and directed only to "good for you" reading material, they may find the alternatives more attractive and lose out on the benefits of reading.

Pleasure reading is a safe way to explore risky behavior and unfamiliar ideas. When reading is self-selected, the teen can simply put it down if it becomes too much. Everyone has a point at which a risk or idea in a book stops being exciting and boundary stretching and becomes uncomfortable. Interestingly, when teens talk about the appropriateness of various titles, they are quick to note that what was fine for them at sixteen would not be something that they would want a younger teen to read. We have observed that when teens read something that pushes a boundary too far, few will hesitate to discard it in favor of something more comfortable. Often, though, they will label the book boring or totally unrealistic or just weird rather than too violent or too grim or the like. Parents are sometimes concerned about the ideas that their teens may get from the material they read. Dealing with sensitive subjects will be discussed further in chapter 7, but in the meantime it is crucial to remember that when selecting reading material teens typically seek information, escapism, or connection and that pushing boundaries and returning to a safe and familiar environment is of paramount importance in adolescence.

Reading for Entertainment

All the while teens are reading and gaining information, finding connections with others and affirmation of themselves, escaping into a fascinating story, or challenging their boundaries, they are also enjoying one of the great benefits of reading that any avid reader, regardless of age, can relate to: they are having fun. It is thrilling to sit in on discussions of hot new books during our teen advisory board meetings when the participants' reactions to certain characters or plot twists become so exuberant that we get odd looks from patrons passing by the meeting room. The message boards of popular teen authors such as Rachel Cohn (*Gingerbread, The Steps*), Darren Shan (*Cirque du Freak*), or Ned Vizzini (*Teen Angst? Naaah . . . , Be More Chill*) provide uplifting and enlightening insights into the enthusiasm that teens have for the books they are reading. Even without the overwhelming body of evidence showing that reading is academically and socially beneficial, it would surely be worthwhile to encourage an activity that provides enjoyment, can be sustained throughout life, and introduces new opportunities and ideas.

In *Reading Matters: What the Research Reveals about Reading, Libraries, and Community*, the authors found that avid adult readers often relate the importance of reading in their life to that of breathing.[15] Many adults can recall the book that turned them into readers, or the summer that they discovered Hunter S. Thompson or Jane Austen, or the time they mentioned a book to a classmate and as a result made a lifelong friend. Reading is a habit and hobby and way of life that most people seem to develop when they are young. It is a seed planted early in life that, if nurtured through adolescence, can flourish and bloom, enriching one's life beyond decades. A librarian does much to develop lifelong readers by helping teens find material that they want to read and by feeding their interests rather than walking them down a proscribed path of Great Books that *should* enrich their lives. When looking at the rationale for providing excellent readers' advisory service to teens, the most important reason lies inside most of us. Reading is important because it just *is*.

....

Notes

1. A. E. Cunningham and K. E. Stanovich, "What Reading Does for the Mind," *American Educator* 22, no. 1 (Spring/Summer 1998): 8–15. K. E. Stanovich and A. E. Cunningham, "Studying the Consequences of Literacy within a Literate Society: The Cognitive Correlates of Print Exposure," *Memory and Cognition* 20, no. 1 (1992): 51–68.

2. Stephen D. Krashen, *The Power of Reading: Insights from the Research*, 2nd ed. (Westport, CT: Libraries Unlimited, 2006), 26.

3. Ibid., 35–37.

4. Marilyn A. Nippold, Jill K. Duthie, and Jennifer Larsen, "Literacy as a Leisure Activity: Free-Time Preferences of Older Children and Young Adults," *Language, Speech, and Hearing Services in Schools* 36 (2005): 93–102.

5. Joanne Ujiie and Stephen Krashen, "Home Run Books and Reading Enjoyment," *Knowledge Quest* 31, no. 1 (2002): 36–37.

6. Paulette M. Rothbauer, "Young Adults and Reading," in *Reading Matters: What the Research Reveals about Reading, Libraries, and Community*, by Catherine Sheldrick Ross, Lynne McKechnie, and Paulette M. Rothbauer (Westport, CT: Libraries Unlimited, 2006), 105.

7. For a rundown on the virtues and demise of *Sassy*, see http://www.salon.com/media/media961118.html.

8. SmartGirl.org, "Latest Survey Results: Report on Teen Read Week 2005," http://www.smartgirl.org/reports/5100284.html. In 2005, "assigned reading" was the third most popular reading choice in the *SmartGirl* survey. In 2006, the third most reported choice was "material found on websites" (SmartGirl.org, "Latest Survey Results: Tell Us What You Think about Reading; Teen Read Week 2006 Summary," http://www.smartgirl.org/reports/6667333.html).

9. "Gayety.net Literature Reviews," http://gayety.net/reviews/literature/boy_meets_boy/.

10. Youa T., "Sisterhood of the Traveling Pants," *Teen Ink: Book Reviews Written by Teens*, http://teenink.com/Past/2005/June/19203.html.

11. Entry on Sarah Dessen's Virtual Guestbook, February 14, 2006, http://htmlgear.tripod.com/guest/control.guest?u=remy010&i=2&a=view.

12. Information and a list of the 40 Developmental Assets are available at the Search Institute's website, http://www.search-institute.org.

13. Margaret Mackey, "Risk, Safety, and Control in Young People's Reading Experiences," *School Libraries Worldwide* 9, no. 1 (2003): 50–63.

14. Mackey, "Risk, Safety, and Control," 50. Internal quotation from Beverly Cleary, *Ramona Forever* (New York: Morrow, 1984), 182.

15. Catherine Sheldrick Ross, Lynne McKechnie, and Paulette M. Rothbauer, *Reading Matters: What the Research Reveals about Reading, Libraries, and Community* (Westport, CT: Libraries Unlimited, 2006), 160.

Part Two

● ● ● ● ● ● ● ● ● ● ● ● ● ● ●

Foundations

3

What Is Readers' Advisory, and Why Is Readers' Advisory for Teens Different?

Familiarity with the basic concepts and services involved in readers' advisory for adults is required in order to understand how to adapt readers' advisory services for teens. Once we have gained skills in the standard practice of readers' advisory, we can tailor our approach and services to the developmental needs of our teen patrons.

This chapter will present

- A brief introduction to the basic concepts and services of readers' advisory
- The anatomy of a readers' advisory encounter
- Tips for adapting adult readers' advisory concepts to improve teen readers' advisory services

Basic Concepts of Readers' Advisory Services

Readers' advisory is more than just passing on suggestions of good books. It is a skill that is part science and part art, with a healthy dash of mind reading. The science comes in the classification of various types of books into genres and categories, grouping them together in a useful and meaningful way, and knowing where and why any given book fits into that scheme. The art of readers' advisory involves masterfully articulating various elements of a book to pique interest and entice the prospective reader. And mind reading definitely can help in detecting just what a patron means when he says he wants "just anything good."

Fortunately, strategies and resources are available to assist those of us who are not part of the Psychic Friends Network to build our skills in the art and science of readers' advisory. This chapter will provide an overview of the concepts of readers' advisory, although it can only skim the surface of very deep water. Those who seek a more comprehensive introduction or a more in-depth look at effective readers' advisory techniques for adults are encouraged to see Joyce Saricks's *Readers' Advisory Service in the Public Library*.[1] For those who are serious about establishing or expanding a readers' advisory service or are seeking to improve their own readers' advisory skills, Saricks's book is an indispensable resource.

Reference for Recreational Reading

The simplest way I have found to explain readers' advisory to those unfamiliar with the concept is to liken it to reference work for recreational reading. When working with teens, you may often have the opportunity to do readers' advisory for homework assignments. This is not exactly recreational reading, but the same concepts and practices apply (see chapter 8). As with reference work, patrons approach the desk seeking information or can be spotted with a perplexed look wandering the floor. Also as with reference work, you will need to conduct an interview to ascertain exactly what type of information the patron is looking for. And most important, as with reference work, you will suggest a variety of materials based on what the patron has asked for, not what you think the patron should have. Thus, a readers' advisory exchange can be broken down into three distinct parts: the approach, the interview, and the presentation of options and resolution. This is true whether you work with teens or adults, though when working with teens, you may need to make some minor stylistic adjustments to traditional readers' advisory services.

The Approach

Quite obviously, the key to a successful approach phase is to be approachable. Because some patrons may assume that librarians do not want to be bothered or that only serious informational reference questions merit attention, they never take advantage of readers' advisory services, even though they would benefit from or enjoy them. Some patrons may approach us and describe exactly what they want, but far more patrons will look for a book on their own and not think to ask at the service desk. Many library patrons do not realize that asking for help in finding a good book for leisure reading is completely legitimate and even encouraged. We can work to change this misconception by focusing on our approachability. Welcoming facial expressions, acknowledging patrons when they enter our area, and offering assistance are great starts.

Because teens see us as authority figures (or at the very least, as adults), approachability and an open, positive attitude are of utmost importance. Remember that teens often face challenges in obtaining good customer service based solely on their age and appearance. Their resulting wariness of age bias will often carry over into their interactions with library staff. This is not to say that inappropriate behavior should be tolerated in hopes that teens will see us as cool and come to us for reading suggestions. But acknowledging societal preconceptions that teens face can help inform the manner in which we approach them.

When offering assistance to teens, being specific about what you can offer is often more helpful than a general offer. You could simply ask, "Can I help you?" or "Did you find what you were looking for?" But by observing a teen's behavior (see fig. 3-1) and tailoring your response to that specific situation, you can often initiate a fruitful readers' advisory conversation. For example, if a patron has picked up a teen chick lit title, you can start off by saying, "You know, a lot of people who liked that book are also reading books by this other author." If someone is browsing the new fiction, you can clarify

Figure 3-1 • Reading Your Teens
• •

No one wants to be like the pushy salesperson who lunges at customers the minute they walk into the store, yet our teens need to know that we are serious about our offers of help. The clues below will help you determine which teens to approach and which are content browsing on their own.

Approach if a teen

- Is alone
- Is browsing books and talking about books with a friend or parent
- Is "lingering," meandering through the stacks, soaking it all in
- Picks books up and skims through them, reads flyleaves, and so forth
- Is browsing pathfinders, reading articles posted in the area, or otherwise absorbing materials
- Makes eye contact with or smiles at you when you are in the area

Wait until next time if a teen

- Is just hanging out and socializing with friends
- Is engrossed in reading
- Avoids eye contact
- Is wearing earphones
- Is browsing an area with sensitive materials and does not exhibit any of the above signs of approachability

the type of help you can offer by remarking, "If you don't spot one that looks good, I would be happy to help with some suggestions." Because teen patrons may not be familiar with the services we can provide, offering assistance with specific tasks can let teens know that we have skills from which they can benefit and that we are willing to help.

At our readers' advisory desk, we have many read-alike booklists and other thematic lists available, and we are close to a web public access catalog (PAC). Readers' advisory interviews may begin when teens are browsing the lists and we ask if they are looking for a particular list that we could help them locate. Teens who do not know how to find what they are looking for are often drawn to these printed aids, so they may say something like, "No, nothing in particular, I just can't remember the name of the book my friend suggested." Or when a teen is lingering over the web PAC, we may approach and offer specific help, either with navigating the catalog or by suggesting a book if general keyword searches are not fruitful. These are wonderful openings for a readers' advisory interview.

In our library, the new fiction section is very close to the readers' advisory desk. Because of this configuration, we are able to initiate many readers' advisory interactions while sitting at the desk. However, the new fiction is only a small fraction of the collection as a whole, and that section is not the place to find most browsing teens. Good practice involves seeking out patrons who may be in need of help or might be open to but unaware of readers' advisory services. To find them, move out from behind the desk now and then and take a stroll through the fiction area. You may encounter a patron staring at her favorite author's shelf, lamenting the fact that there are no titles she has not already read and not knowing which other authors she might enjoy. Or you may run into someone who has not been in the library since he did his third-grade state report but has some free time, wants to read some fiction, and does not know where to start. At the same time, you might come across patrons who value their silent wanderings in the stacks and want nothing to do with suggestions or readers' advisors. Whatever the case, we have found that the positive results gained from approaching patrons far outweigh the occasional negative reaction. This concept is particularly important in teen readers' advisory, especially if your library's teen area does not have a service desk. More about initiating a readers' advisory interview will be discussed in chapter 5. The key concepts to keep in mind are summarized in figure 3-2.

The Interview

Any librarian familiar with reference interview techniques will be able to adapt those techniques to a teen readers' advisory interview. Like a reference interview, a readers' advisory interview can include

**Figure 3-2 ● All You _Really_ Need to Know about the Approach Phase
in a Readers' Advisory Interaction**

. . . .

1. Be present. Move out from behind the desk. Patrons rarely linger around the service desk—they want to be where the books are. That is where you also should be in order to offer the help that they need.

2. Be approachable. Smile and let your patrons know that you are happy that they are in your area.

3. Be specific in offering help. "Can I help you?" works only if a patron knows what kind of help is available.

---

such behaviors as active listening, repeating information as you understand it ("So, you're looking for an author who writes like Fannie Flagg but isn't Southern?"), asking open-ended questions, and maintaining objectivity and withholding judgment.[2] However, because of the highly individual nature of reading interests, readers' advisory interviews are more effective when conducted in a conversational style rather than in the methodically structured manner that works so well in reference interviewing. Saricks describes a readers' advisory interview as "a conversation, with readers telling the readers' advisor about books and their leisure-reading tastes and the readers' advisor listening and suggesting possible titles."[3] She goes on to explain that this conversation can be more important than finding the perfect book because it establishes in the patron's mind that discussing leisure reading is a welcome and rewarding activity to engage in with librarians.

During the interview, the librarian should try to use appeal factors, as presented in figure 3-3, to ascertain just what type of book the patron is looking for. Appeal factors do not speak specifically to the content of a book but rather to the elements that a reader may be drawn to or repelled from. In addition to its story line, a book's language, pacing, setting, characterization of people and situations, and "discussability" all contribute to a reader's enjoyment. In fact, a novel with a plot that differs greatly from a reader's typical interests could still be enjoyable if other appeal factors draw the reader in.

Everyone knows the saying, "You can't judge a book by its cover," but equally wise is the idea that you cannot judge a book by its plot. The way an author tells a story can be just as compelling as the story itself—or more so. Literature's great plot lines are recycled again and again, but what keeps them alive, in part, is the artistry the author lends to the tale. Consider the following descriptions of a book whose plot sounded as if it could not be further from my interests but that I absolutely loved because it contained appeal factors that I look for.

Figure 3-3 ● **The Vocabulary of Appeal**

Using the terms below during a readers' advisory interview can help you identify the factors that contribute to a teen's preferences in leisure reading.

Pacing

breakneck, compelling, deliberate, densely written, easy, engrossing, fast paced, leisurely paced, measured, relaxed, stately, unhurried

Characterization

detailed, distant, dramatic, eccentric, evocative, faithful, familiar, intriguing secondary (characters), introspective, lifelike, multiple points of view, quirky, realistic, recognizable, series (characters), vivid, well developed, well drawn

Story Line

action oriented, character centered, complex, domestic, episodic, explicit violence, family centered, folksy, gentle, inspirational, issue oriented, layered, literary references, multiple plotlines, mystical, mythic, open ended, plot centered, plot twists, racy, resolved ending, rich and famous, romp, sexually explicit, steamy, strong language, thought-provoking, tragic

Frame and Tone

bittersweet, bleak, contemporary, darker (tone), detailed setting, details of [insert an area of specialized knowledge or skill], edgy, evocative, exotic, foreboding, gritty, hard edged, heartwarming, historical details, humorous, lush, magical, melodramatic, menacing, mystical, nightmare (tone), nostalgic, philosophical, political, psychological, romantic, rural, sensual, small town, stark, suspenseful, timeless, upbeat, urban

Style

austere, candid, classic, colorful, complex, concise, conversational, direct, dramatic, elaborate, elegant, extravagant, flamboyant, frank, graceful, homespun, jargon, metaphorical, natural, ornate, poetic, polished, prosaic, restrained, seemly, showy, simple, sophisticated, stark, thoughtful, unaffected, unembellished, unpretentious, unusual

Source: Joyce G. Saricks, *Readers' Advisory Service in the Public Library,* 3rd ed. (Chicago: ALA Editions, 2005), 66.

Plot-based description: Orson Scott Card's *Ender's Game* is a science fiction story about a young boy recruited into a futuristic military training school as the last great hope for saving the world from an evil alien race.

Appeal-based description: Orson Scott Card's *Ender's Game* is full of strong, relatable, and complex characters. It is told from multiple perspectives with moderate pacing, though it does have several fast-paced action sequences as well. Part family drama, part adventure, part coming-of-age story, it is a unique and provocative novel providing much fodder for discussion.

Given the plot-based description alone, readers may expect a breakneck-paced, action-packed, plot-driven story told in short chapters and may be surprised by the sometimes contemplative tone or the philosophical and political issues dealt with in parts of *Ender's Game*. In contrast, without mentioning the plot at all, the appeal-based description provides enough information for prospective readers to judge if the book sounds like what they are looking for. They may still be turned off by the plot, but knowing what the appeal factors are will give them a sense of what the *experience* of reading the book will be like.

The key concepts to keep in mind during the interview phase of a readers' advisory interaction are summarized in figure 3-4.

The Presentation of Options

When presenting the fruits of our readers' advisory labor to a patron, it is useful to keep in mind two of S. R. Ranganathan's laws of library science:[4]

**Figure 3-4 • All You *Really* Need to Know about the Interview Phase in a
Readers' Advisory Interaction**

. . . .

1. Exhibit good interview behaviors, such as active listening and asking both open-ended and specific questions, to get to the root of the patron's request.

2. Speak in a conversational style to help patrons understand that you are happy to discuss leisure reading and that you welcome their return for future readers' advisory services.

3. Use appeal factors when asking patrons about their preferences as well as when describing potential reads.

Law number 2: Every reader his or her book.
Law number 4: Save the time of the reader.

Law number 2 could be a readers' advisory motto. We must believe that there is a book out there for each reader. It is not always easy to find that book, but we have better luck if, rather than trying to find exactly the right book ourselves, we use information from the readers' advisory interview to offer the patron several options and allow the patron to determine the most suitable book. Finding that book may take several tries, especially when you are working with teens or patrons who have particular likes or dislikes. Using the tools and guides discussed later in this book will help greatly in narrowing down the choices, but doing so can still take time. When working on a particularly difficult request or helping a patron who seems to have a reading interest that you just cannot meet, remember rule number 4. As tricky and time-consuming as the request may be, you can achieve a much faster result than the patron could by wandering up and down the aisles.

You can also save a patron time by pulling several books off the shelf and allowing her to peruse them. Using the basic plot points and clearest appeal factors, give the patron a thirty-second booktalk before leaving her to choose from the titles you have selected. Often, when a patron mentions a particular title she enjoyed, we can use that as a point of reference. For example, if a patron is looking for something to read after having enjoyed Carolyn Mackler's *The Earth, My Butt, and Other Big Round Things*, the books pulled can be related to that title. Megan McCafferty's *Sloppy Firsts* is similar, but lighter and more focused on friends and dating than on the family. Or Kathleen Jeffrie Johnson's *The Parallel Universe of Liars* could be described as similar in that the main character is also on her own in figuring out who she can rely on and how she feels about those around her. The great joy in readers' advisory comes when, weeks or even months after a conversation with a patron, she returns to your desk to tell you that you found *the* book that speaks to her.

Librarians should attempt, to the best of their ability, to find the type of book the patron has requested, even if they may not personally enjoy or appreciate that type of fiction. Connecting the process of readers' advisory to good reference practices, if a patron approached the reference desk asking for information on how to obtain a divorce, the librarian would not give him something called *Every Marriage Can Be Saved*. The librarian would of course be seen as imposing a personal view on a patron, which would be inappropriate. Recreational reference—readers' advisory—is no different. This is an especially important concept for readers' advisory work with teens. The key concepts to keep in mind when presenting options based on a readers' advisory interview are summarized in figure 3-5.

Teens are constantly being told what they should do—from what to wear, to how to do their schoolwork, to how to improve their general behavior.

Figure 3-5   ●   All You *Really* Need to Know about Presenting Options after a Readers' Advisory Interview

. . . .

1. Remember that there *is* a book out there for every patron, even if it takes a while to find it.

2. Save the reader's time by giving brief descriptions of the books after pulling them off the shelves to hand to your patron.

3. Listen to what the patron is asking for and try to give her just that, reserving judgment of the literary value of the request. The goal in readers' advisory for leisure reading is to give the patron what she wants to read, not what you think that she *should* read.

The bulk of this, one hopes, comes from well-intentioned adults who care about teens and want to see them succeed. One great way to help teens succeed in life is to help instill in them a love of and an interest in reading. But that cannot be achieved by attempting to foist good-for-you books on blossoming readers. Instead, readers' advisory for teens functions on the concept that reading of any kind in any genre is valid and should be encouraged. So when a young teen comes looking for a romantic book, steering her to Jane Austen's *Emma* because it fits the description, or to Margaret Mitchell's *Gone with the Wind* because you loved it at her age, should probably not be your first, or at least your only, response.

Concluding the Readers' Advisory Interaction

Once you have presented various options to the patron, end the readers' advisory interaction in a way that invites future contact. Even if the patron did not want to engage in a lengthy conversation about finding a book, saying that if he needs help next time, you would be happy to make a suggestion can go a long way in establishing the library as a friendly place in which to discuss fiction and recreational reading.

Sometimes a patron's request really strikes a chord or is so open ended that the options could be limitless, and you may find yourself giving the patron more books than he is ready for at the moment. In situations like this, it is important to give the patron—especially a teen patron—an out. This lets him know that the choice of what to check out is up to him and that you will give him as many or as few suggestions as he feels he needs. Pay attention to the patron's attentiveness and body language. If you see an overwhelmed, eyes-glazed-over look, take a moment and give him a graceful way to end the conversation (see fig. 3-6). You may be pleasantly surprised to hear that the patron really could

Figure 3-6 ● Open-Ended Ways to End a Readers' Advisory Conversation

- If you take a look at these and they aren't what you want, just let me know and I'll be happy to try again.
- We'll be here if you need help finding something next time.
- Next time you're in, let us know what you thought of the book.
- Do you feel that you have enough suggestions, or would you like me to pull a few more possibilities?
- Have I overloaded you yet, or could you use a few more titles?
- Do any of these books sound interesting, or should I pull some different options?

use just one more book or that he thinks that the first one you mentioned is exactly what he is looking for. On the other hand, you may discover that what you thought the request was and what the patron actually wants are very different things. This pause in the conversation will allow you to change directions and also lets the patron know that his interests really do matter, that you are hearing what he is asking for and doing your best to give it to him.

What Makes Teens So Different?

Readers' advisory for teenagers differs from readers' advisory for adults not just in the selection of materials that we offer but also in the manner in which we conduct ourselves. Whereas an easy rapport may form between two adults discussing a book, we must remain aware that because teens most often encounter adults as teachers, parents, or supervisors, they may be caught off guard or surprised by our usual manner, be it poised professionalism or more laid-back joviality. Though we need not handle our teen patrons with kid gloves, being aware that emotional volatility is part and parcel of adolescent development may help our interactions, especially when we have trouble understanding or communicating ideas. Just as we might kneel down to speak to a toddler or raise our voice to speak to someone who is hard of hearing, adjusting our manner to meet the developmental stage of teenagers can lead to a more effective readers' advisory interview all around. Consider the following:

> The words that we speak make up only 7 percent of what a listener believes about our message; the remaining 93 percent is influenced by tone of voice (38 percent) and nonverbal cues (55 percent).[5]

Sarcasm or good-natured teasing can work against congruent com-munication—communication that avoids conflict and allows feelings to be expressed—which has been shown to be most effective with teens. It can easily be viewed as criticism when the intent may be completely benign.[6]

Teens and adults read and interpret facial expressions with different parts of their brains. The prefrontal cortex, the part of the brain that most accurately deciphers facial expressions, is the part that adults use for this task. However, in teens the prefrontal cortex is still developing. In its stead, the amygdala—sharply attuned to emotional responses such as fear—interprets facial expressions.[7] The difference can lead to misunderstandings because the adolescent brain does not yet interpret subtle facial expressions in the most accurate way, nor does it interpret them through the same mechanisms as an adult brain.

Teens view respect, sharing of time, and openness as the three most important ways in which adults can show that they are interested in providing help.[8]

The research on the way that adolescents absorb messages indicates that we can best communicate with teens by being clearer and more direct than we might be with adult patrons. We need to make extra efforts in our readers' advisory conversations to display our attention to and interest in what teens are asking for and saying. Our body language and facial expressions should reinforce the sentiments we express as clearly as possible. Due to the unique developmental qualities of adolescence, active and empathetic listening becomes more important when working with teens. We need to allow teens to express their ideas or interests before offering interpretations or asking clarifying questions. While teens are talking, we need to focus fully on what they are asking or telling us and resist the temptation to do catalog searches or write down names of authors and books that we are itching to tell them about. We need to devote at least the same amount and quality of time to our teen patrons as we would to our adult patrons, And most important, we need to show genuine respect for our teen patrons—their likes and dislikes, their reading interests and aversions, and their personal qualities—to demonstrate that we *are* helping adults who want to assist them in finding recreational reading.

Conclusion

Readers' advisory can both bring great pleasure to our patrons and be a challenging and enjoyable activity for staff. Though it may appear to require a daunting amount of knowledge, be consoled that every book or review we read and every conversation about books that we have increases our skill. It is easy to be intimidated when observing skilled readers' advisors working with patrons—it really does appear that they are mind readers at times! However, the people who make readers' advisory look easy usually have years of experience in its art and science. Remember that at the core of the service is a conversation about books. Whether you are working with adults or teenagers, the skills are the same. However, given teens' perceptions and sensitivities, you may need to adapt your conversation style a bit. Through active listening and careful practice, anyone who has the desire to give high-quality readers' advisory service will be able to do so.

Notes

1. Joyce G. Saricks, *Readers' Advisory Service in the Public Library*, 3rd ed. (Chicago: ALA Editions, 2005).

2. Reference and User Service Association, "Guidelines for Behavioral Performance of Reference and Information Service Providers" (2004), http://www.ala.org/ala/rusa/rusaprotools/referenceguide/guidelinesbehavioral.htm.

3. Saricks, *Readers' Advisory Service in the Public Library*, 75.

4. G. Edward Evans, Anthony J. Amodeo, and Thomas L. Carter, *Introduction to Library Public Services*, 6th ed. (Greenwood, CO: Libraries Unlimited, 1999), 280. Ranganathan's laws: (1) Books are for use; (2) Every reader his book; (3) Every book its reader; (4) Save the time of the reader; (5) A library is a growing organism.

5. Paul W. Swets, *The Art of Talking with Your Teenager* (Holbrook, MA: Adams Media Corporation, 1995), 38–39.

6. Dave F. Brown, "The Significance of Congruent Communication in Effective Classroom Management," *The Clearing House* 79 (September/October 2005): 13–14.

7. David Walsh, *Why Do They Act That Way?* (New York: Free Press, 2004), 77–78.

8. June Martin, Michael Romas, Marsha Medford, Nancy Leffert, and Sherry L. Hatcher, "Adult Helping Qualities Preferred by Adolescents," *Adolescence* 41 (Spring 2006): 127–38. The additional qualities teens expressed as being most important were, in order, role characteristics, recognition, guidance, identification, trust, freedom, like/dislike, responsibility, and familiarity.

4

Tips for the Generalist

What to Do If You Have Not Read Teen Fiction Since You Were a Teen

To provide high-quality readers' advisory service to teens, it is important to be familiar with literature for young adults and what distinguishes it from literature for children or adults. This chapter will explain how to learn about young adult fiction and suggest resources directed at individuals who aspire to be teen readers' advisors but may lack the background to do an outstanding job.

This chapter will cover

- How and where to read reviews and use resources
- Genres in teen literature to be aware of
- Where to begin reading to familiarize yourself with teen literature

A Journey of a Thousand Miles . . .

Most librarians in public and school libraries have to wear many hats. Perhaps you typically work the reference desk and would like to branch out into YA librarianship, or you are familiar with adult fiction readers' advisory but have recently realized the potential in improving YA readers' advisory. Congratulations. You have made a great decision that will improve the library experience of the young people in your area and your professional marketability, and it is possible you will find a new favorite book or two along the way. This chapter is intended to lay out a basic plan for familiarizing yourself with this new territory, the first step in your journey of a thousand miles. Take heart, you do not need to know every book in the YA collection to do YA readers' advisory, just as you do not need to know all about bass fishing in order to help a patron who is looking for a good book on bass fishing. However, knowing about your collection and having a few personal favorite authors or titles in mind will help you to assist patrons and communicate that their questions about teen literature are valid and welcome.

Think back to the last young adult book you read. Was it a Hardy Boys or Nancy Drew mystery you read under the covers with a flashlight? A hot-off-the-presses copy of Judy Blume's *Forever* or Lois Duncan's *Stranger with My Face*? Did you check it out of your own high school library, or buy it with lawn-mowing money? Or maybe you did not realize such a class of literature existed until you were well out of your own teenage years and are just now realizing how much has been written over the past years that is waiting on a bookshelf for you to discover—or waiting in a warehouse for you to purchase for your library. It is not an insurmountable task to familiarize oneself with young adult literature, and it is not too late to jump on the bandwagon. In fact, right now is the perfect time. We are widely considered to be in the second golden age of young adult literature, so there is no lack of great titles to read. And after all—as time passes, there will be more YA books to discover and more young people will have passed through the library without the guidance that you could have offered them.

What Is Young Adult Literature?

As you delve into the wide range of books specifically created for young adults, remember that more likely than not, you already know a few titles that would be great reads for teens—some adult fiction, science fiction and fantasy, cult classics, and popular nonfiction are widely read by teenagers, especially older teens. Think back to the books that you may have heard teens ask about at the desk or books that you may have read and thought that a teenage acquaintance might enjoy. Chances are, these are very diverse books about a wide range of characters and topics, with varied narrative devices. Thinking about the diversity of adult fiction reminds us that teen fiction is not all the same, just as its readers are not all the same (see fig. 4-1).

Figure 4-1 ● **General Qualities That Identify Much of Young Adult Literature**

1. The protagonist is a teenager, as are most of the key players.
2. The protagonist is close to the experiences, not reflecting back on time gone by as an adult.
3. The book's issues and conflicts are relevant to the life of a teenager.

Teens read a wide variety of materials in addition to YA fiction, from classics to paperback romances, to *New York Times* best sellers and more. However, fictional works specifically intended for young adults typically share at least a few distinguishing characteristics and it is those works that I will refer to as YA literature.

There are many qualities commonly found in YA literature. First-person narration, a literal or perceived absence of one or both parents, a coming-of-age, lots of dialogue, a relatively low page count, and the use of slang are all attributes of many YA novels. However, one quality stands out from all the others and is most useful in distinguishing young adult literature from literature that young adults choose to read: characters close in age to the reader with perspectives that are true to the experiences and interpretations of real teenagers.

Teenage characters are not unique to YA literature. What is unique is the perspective of the character involved in the story. In YA literature, the teen protagonist is emotionally and temporally close to the experiences of being a teenager. In contrast, a story about a teenager as recalled by an adult woman reflecting on "that summer" or a third-person narrative that portrays teens reacting to life rather than functioning as active agents would not qualify as YA literature because the storytellers are too far removed from the events. Consider, for example, Chris Bohjalian's *Midwives*, which is narrated by Connie, a fourteen-year-old whose mother is on trial. Although the novel might be popular with teens, it is not a YA novel because the story is told not as Connie is living it day by day but as she reflects back on that time in her life through the perspective of an adult woman who has had time to think the situation over and come to certain understandings. This is a key difference between YA literature and other literature. When a YA novel is told in the past tense, the narration still has a sense of immediacy about it. The reader gets the feeling that the characters have just experienced the events, not that they are recalling their youth. Especially in adventure stories, the temporal setup often takes the tone of "Listen to what I've just been through" rather than "Listen to what happened to my grandfather when he was a teenager."

The plots in many novels for adults unfold slowly over the years, but the action in YA literature tends to be much more acute, taking place in a matter of weeks or months. After all, while adults may refer to stages of their lives in terms of decades, each grade level brings a new stage for teenagers as they progress from middle-schoolers to high school freshmen, on up to the coveted status of high school seniors, each stage with its own unique concerns, privileges, and rites of passage. Characters in YA lit tend to age very little because the developmental phases are so much more condensed than those of an adult. Aging a youngster by as little as two years—say, from twelve to fourteen or from sixteen to eighteen—could result in a character whose concerns, abilities, and perspectives vastly change from the beginning of the novel to the end. The immediacy of a character's experience within his or her age group and developmental stage is one of the hallmarks of YA lit. Standard time frames for YA literature are the three months of summer or the nine months of a school year, though of course some take place in much briefer slices of time as well.

The exception to this is in YA books that begin with a young character who ages quickly up to the point when the main action of the story begins. This is often found in novels with fantastical elements, as readers may need more backstory in order to understand the main character's world and frame of mind. Sally Gardner's historical fantasy *I, Coriander,* for example, introduces the reader to a six-year-old protagonist who comes upon a magical pair of shoes, among other unusual situations. Through the course of the story she ages to fifteen, and because of her early brushes with the fairy world she is able to contextualize and understand the circumstances she later encounters. Likewise, the first Harry Potter novel follows Harry from birth to age eleven within the span of mere pages, with each subsequent book taking place over the course of a school year.[1]

Many novels dealing with young protagonists have some element of coming-of-age, or learning and growing from experiences. The perspective of a YA novel differs from many adult novels with regard to this plot line. Novels written specifically for teens tend to let the reader move through the journey of discovery with the characters. The narrative is often structured to let the reader learn and discover with the character, as opposed to having the broader perspective found in many adult novels. Liesa Abrams, an editor of YA books, reminds writers that "adults commonly express the sentiment that the drama and heartache of their teen years were unrealistically magnified. But for teens who are living it, it's every bit as real as it feels. Be careful, in general," she warns, "that characters don't think with adult attitudes."[2] A well-crafted YA novel truly carries the perspective of a teen, not the view of an adult who remembers being a teen or an adult's perception of how a teen should feel.

Librarians working with young adult literature are well served by applying Abrams's advice as they read, critique, and suggest books to teens. A comment I have heard on occasion from those unfamiliar with contemporary YA lit is that it just seems so facile; its characters seem to be occupied by such silly teenage drama. While this might apply to some YA lit, it is crucial to remember what those years were really like—when having the right shade of blue in your jeans, or getting bumped from first trumpet to second, or being on the receiving end of a slightly off look from the person who occupied your thoughts day and night, or being the one to score the winning point really and truly were earth-shattering issues and moments.

Another comment from those new to reading YA lit might be that the scenarios do not seem realistic: Why would someone act the way the protagonist acted when an alternative solution would have "made much more sense"? It is helpful for us to remember that the thought processes and actions of teenagers are not always the same as those of adults. This should not excuse shoddy storytelling—far from it in fact. The storytelling needs to capture the thought processes of the teenager who is living in a particular situation. Someone with the benefit of experience would recognize that Casey in Audrey Couloumbis's *Say Yes* should have immediately called in the authorities when she realized that her missing guardian was not coming back. However, for a twelve-year-old who had lost all of the important people in her life, her reaction—to hide the situation and try to stay in the place she knows—is very understandable.

One of the great treasures that reading offers is the chance to step into the world of another person. When reading YA literature as adults, not only do we have the opportunity to experience a new place, time period, or situation, but we also gain a more personally relevant glimpse back in time. We are offered the opportunity either to revisit the point of view of our own teenage years or to journey into a teen experience that is foreign to us. This is only slightly different from reading about adult characters who are different from us. We might be intrigued by the culture, community, and way of life in Precious Ramotswe's Botswana from Alexander McCall Smith's *The No. 1 Ladies' Detective Agency*, and we may find that the landscape of a contemporary YA novel is just as foreign to us. Until, that is, the moment that the ground shifts and we are transported back into our own shoes at eighteen. At that point, the author of the well-crafted YA novel not only has given adult readers a chance to experience a different place or time but also has presented us the opportunity to experience the emotions and perspectives of our own teenage years once again.

Starting to Read Young Adult Fiction: Setting a Reading Plan

Knowing what YA literature is and having a basic familiarity with its popular genres and authors give the readers' advisor a great foundation for understanding and talking about these books with teens. There are several ways in which to develop your expertise. More and more courses on YA literature are being offered in library schools. The YALSA

Professional Development Center online offers syllabi of several such courses in order to aid librarians "thrust into the role of young adult librarian without any type of pre-service training" in structuring educational programs for themselves.[3] Resource guides like *Teen Genreflecting* or *A Core Collection for Young Adults* provide excellent information about the important works in YA fiction and other popular formats for teens.[4] Another useful tool is the Young Adult Genre Fiction List produced by the Adult Reading Round Table (ARRT) in Illinois.[5] This useful compilation includes definitions of popular YA genres as well as lists of stand-out authors and titles within each genre. Those already working in libraries are surrounded by very useful and informative tools—the space, materials, and teens in your own library. Whichever method you choose, it is important to structure your reading plan to provide both broad and deep coverage of the most popular and most important works in YA lit today.

Setting a reading plan for yourself will give your study of YA literature focus and purpose. If your goal is to prepare yourself or your coworkers to conduct readers' advisory for teens, your reading plan should include books that span a broad range of interests and reading levels, which will equip you to work with teen readers in general, as well as books that suit the specific interests and reading levels of your library's teen patrons. Consider the type of facility in which you intend to conduct your readers' advisory service. Is it a public library? A middle or high school library? Does your library have a special collection that is particularly popular with teens, such as manga, popular nonfiction, or paperback series? Are teens in your area interested in a specific genre, such as urban, inspirational, or horror fiction? Due to these and many other variables, it is impossible to compile a single all-encompassing, one-size-fits-all reading plan. The popular authors lists in appendix A provide starting points for the basic genres, but they must be supplemented with works by authors of local interest and tailored to a particular librarian in a particular situation and community.

Authors Popular with Young Adults

The popular authors lists were inspired by the popular fiction list detailed in the Saricks book *Readers' Advisory Service in the Public Library* and adapted for use in many libraries nationwide. They were created as a training tool for the Downers Grove Public Library's readers' advisory staff and are a growing and changing work. The list as a whole comprises three broad genre lists. Within each broad genre are subgenre lists of five authors each, with the benchmark author listed first and the others following alphabetically. The categories do not apply to the entire body of

YA literature but rather reflect the genres and authors popular at the present time in our particular community. Because YA literature is constantly evolving and the field of authors writing quality literature is quickly expanding, the list must frequently be revisited. The authors on the list were chosen based on several criteria. First, the author should still be producing work, with the singular exception of Robert Cormier, as he remains the benchmark author of teen psychological suspense. Second, the author should have at least two books suitable for teens. And third, the author's work should be highly acclaimed, very popular, or representative of the genre.

The grand total of ninety authors on the popular authors lists are representative of the breadth of YA lit, but they are only a fraction of the many talented, innovative, and popular authors currently writing for teens. Because the lists were created in mid-2006 with a specific public library's teen clientele in mind, they will need to be revised to fit the popular interests of your community and accommodate the emergence of hot new authors. Benchmark authors are listed first in order to help familiarize those new to YA lit with the best and most recognizable authors within each genre. Since many teens will either know of these authors or have read their work, readers' advisory interviews will be more productive if the librarian is familiar with them too. Understanding what kind of book Louise Rennison or Kevin Brooks writes will assist you in narrowing down the field of possible matches when working with a patron.

So Many Books, So Little Time

First, a Word on Keeping Track

Whether you speed read, skim, or read the entire book, keeping a record of what you have read will help recall each book and its appeal elements. If you already have a method for logging books read—keep with it! If you have yet to start a reading log, here are some suggestions for making one work for you.

Use a method that is comfortable for you. If a PDA is your lifeline or if you are never far from your laptop, adding notes in an electronic file may be the way to go. Some people prefer to make handwritten notes in a simple spiral-bound notebook or a hardcover journal. Choosing the form of a reading log, just like choosing a planner or a purse, is very much based on personal taste and intended use. The basic information recorded in a log will be relatively standard from person to person. At the minimalist end of the spectrum is the listing of title, author, and date read. Jotting down a book's genre, a few key words, and a suggested age range will help you recall a book that may not have impressed you but would be perfect for one of your patrons. A more detailed log may include descriptions of characters and setting and an exploration of the book's specific appeal.

Personally, I keep two logs. One is a simple paper journal in which I record title, author, date read, and type of book (adult or teen, fiction or nonfiction, mystery, horror, romance, and so forth). This log jump-starts my memory when I am trying to pull together quick, thematic booklists and is useful in identifying trends in my reading habits. If I look back and see that the past four books I have read mainly appeal to younger teen girls, I can try to switch gears to broaden my reading.

The second log is more detailed, kept in a word processing file, and stored both at work and on a portable flash drive. This log includes a combination of full annotations that are suitable for a booklist and keywords about appeal factors that will help me to write a full annotation at some point in the near future. My reasons for writing annotations are twofold. First, it is much easier to annotate a book when it is fresh in my mind than to go back to it years after the fact. Unless a book was utterly wretched (in which case I log that I read it in my notebook but skip the annotation), I assume that I could pass it on as a suggestion at some point. Why not annotate it sooner rather than later? Second, the task of writing the annotation forces me to process the appeal factors and mold them into something that I can articulate to patrons. Because people do not all process information in the same way, I would not contend that this is the best or the only way to keep records. Ultimately, each reader needs to find the method that is personally most useful and be diligent about following through with it.

Your Personal Reading Plan

As you begin to compile a must-read list of books or authors, it is comforting and important to remember that while you might want to pore over each title from cover to cover, savoring each page, this is not necessary for the time being. Knowing a book is certainly better than knowing about a book, but knowing about fifty books is better than thoroughly knowing only five. Speed reading, skimming, and reading parts of books will increase your knowledge of teen books much more quickly than reading each title with painstaking thoroughness.

Set a goal and timeframe for completing your reading plan, keeping in mind that the reading done to familiarize yourself with a genre or any other group of books is different from reading purely for pleasure. For those of us who are serious readers, it can be a trying task to skim through a book, or to read only the first and last chapters, or to use any other speed-reading techniques. Frequently, while trying to read books on my own lists of genres I want to familiarize myself with, I find myself straying from my time goal because I am caught up in a story. I empathize with others who gasp at the thought of reading a book's last chapter without reading the middle or of simply reading a book's cover and picking out pages here and there to skim. However, it is a useful habit to adopt and allows us the time to focus on really reading and enjoying the titles that we find ourselves especially drawn to. Georgine Olson's guide "Speed Reading Books, or How to Read a Novel in Just Minutes" (fig. 4-2) is a wonderful resource for structuring speed-reading

Figure 4-2 ● Speed Reading Books, or How to Read a Novel in Just Minutes
. . . .

Basics of Speed Reading

1. Select a book to read.
2. On a card, sheet of paper, or form, record the author, title, genre, series info, and call number. As you "read," jot down notes about items listed below that seem pertinent.
3. Hold the book and look at its basic features.
   - Is it heavy?
   - When you open it, do the pages lie flat?
   - Look at the typeface, the space between lines, the general layout—How easy to read is it? Is there much white space? Is it densely printed?
4. Look at the cover—What does it tell you about the book (or what the publisher wants you to think about the book)?
5. Read the blurb—Does it give you an idea of the story line? Does it tell "everything" (or maybe nothing at all)? Is it inviting, teasing, ominous?
6. Read the first chapter—Does it pull you right into the story or is there a slow build-up? If it is a series title, how smoothly does it deliver background info?
7. Skim and read bits and pieces here and there throughout the book—Does it seem to flow? What is your general impression of the book?
8. Read the end (sorry, but this is important!). If it has an epilogue, read a couple of sections before the epilogue. Is there a conclusion to the story or is it open-ended? Does the ending read like a checklist, mechanically wrapping up all loose ends?
9. What can you tell about
   - Style: humorous; serious; length of sentences, sections, or chapters; dialogue
   - Pacing: leisurely or action-oriented
   - Format: straight-line narrative, flashback, single or multiple points of view, smoothness of transitions
   - Characters: many or few, recognizable types, character-oriented or action-oriented
   - Setting: time, place, integral or wallpaper
   - Story line: character driven or plot driven
   - Genre: adherence to genre conventions, recognizable subgenre

Figure 4-2 (cont.)
● ●

From the Readers' Advisor's Viewpoint

1. Does this book bring to mind any other authors or titles as possible read-alikes?

2. Which readers could enjoy this? Why would they?

3. Think about how you would phrase a recommendation based on speed reading versus cover-to-cover reading versus what you might have learned from reviews or other readers.

Becoming Proficient at Speed Reading (and Learning Its Value and Limitations)

1. Practice; set a goal (three books an hour, thirty books a week, or the like).

2. Speed read five books you read and enjoyed a long time ago (at least several years). How much comes back to you? How much of what you are speed reading reminds you of what you so enjoyed the last time you read the book? Are you getting a "feel" for the book? Does it seem like the same book you read before, or does it seem different?

3. Speed read five books that you have not read but would be at the top of your to-read list. Then read the books from cover to cover as you normally would. How different are your impressions of the book: speed reading versus regular reading?

4. Find people (preferably with some knowledge of readers' advisory) who read in a genre you do not read. Ask them to select five newish books in the genre that they have read and enjoyed. Speed read the five books and discuss each with the person who recommended them. How well have you read these?

5. Get together with several others and speed read the same book. Have a mini book discussion to compare your impressions and notes. What is similar and what is different in the various readings of the book? How does this compare with the usual book discussion experience?

Source: Georgine N. Olson, "Speed Reading Books, or How to Read a Novel in Ten Minutes—Readers' Advisory Tool Kit" (presentation, Public Library Association National Conference, Seattle, February 27, 2004; updated November 7, 2005), http://www.ala.org/ala/pla/plaevents/nationalconf/program/fridayprograms/ratoolkit.doc. Reprinted with permission.

with focus. To use this guide, set a goal for the number of books you want to work through within a given time frame. A reasonable goal could be five books a week at the rate of one book a day, read in the ten minutes of your bus ride home, or in the last ten minutes of the workday, or during the free moments you have while working at the desk. If you need more than ten minutes to cover all the points in the guide, give yourself twenty minutes or half an hour. But give yourself a limit and stick to it. Otherwise, you may find yourself spending two hours on a book instead of the ten minutes or so that you had intended. After completing a particular reading goal, reward yourself by reading a book for your own enjoyment—if all of our reading is task oriented, it is easy to start losing the joy that drew us to the world of books in the first place.

The most useful teen books to begin reading are local favorites. These are the titles you are frequently asked about at the desk, those that frequently show up on summer reading lists or in curricula at your local schools, and those that often need replacement or repair for wear and tear. A well-worn book is often a well-loved book. Starting with local favorites will provide immediate benefits both for you as a readers' advisor for teens and for the teens themselves. Imagine a teen who approaches the desk to ask for one of the suggested titles for incoming freshmen. If you have read the book and are able to comment on it, you have a great jumping-off point for a conversation about other similar books, or you may simply establish yourself as an individual at the library who is friendly and open to discussing books with teens.

Because most of us do not have the challenge or opportunity to build a young adult collection from the ground up, we are able to familiarize ourselves with locally popular titles by exploring the space and materials that we already have. Be present in your teen area. Look at the shelves as if you have never seen them before and note what titles jump out at you. This may be a good place to start reading—after all, if you noticed a flashy neon green spine with pink lettering, it is likely that the teens have noticed it as well. Then again, if you pull it from the shelf and find it coated in dust with a spine that appears not to have been cracked in four years, it may be best to start with something else.

Another useful place to browse for titles to add to your list are the shelves or carts of books waiting to be shelved. What better way is there to find out what local teenagers are reading than to look at what they are checking out of the library? Some of the items found will not be surprises. Books recently adapted into movies, required or suggested school reading, long-standing favorites like *Go Ask Alice*, and popular paperback series could make up a large portion of the books checked out.[6] While it is useful to know about these, it is also interesting to familiarize yourself with other titles that appear on the sorting shelves with regularity. These word-of-mouth favorites are treasures for the young adult librarian to come across. They provide reassurance that the books we chose based on reviews or hunches that they would be popular have turned out to be good matches for the teens in our community. These books are also valuable resources because though they may never make a best-of list, be a teacher's summer reading assignment, or be turned into a blockbuster movie, they obviously mean something to teens in your area. Discovering what that is and what to look for in other books is another task entirely and will be discussed further in chapter 6.

Reading Reviews: Why, Where, and How

We are all aware of how constantly changing and evolving the library world is. Just as soon as we have caught up on the newest technology or literary trend, another one might appear, seemingly fully formed, out of the blue. Fortunately, when it comes to keeping tabs on what is happening in YA literature, several sources of reviews are a great help in spotting trends and hot new authors. A librarian who wants to increase service to teens can benefit by reading reviews of teen books in the same way that someone who wants to brush up on local politics would benefit from reading the local paper. If you are the librarian selecting materials for the young adult area, reading reviews of YA books is undoubtedly already part of your daily routine. Even if you are not the selector, you can gain a great deal by reading reviews of YA books in addition to materials in your own selection area. Some hints for getting the most out of reviews are presented in figure 4-3.

Although there are many avenues for exploring new YA literature, I have found the following three sources to be the most useful, and they are readily accessible in many public and school libraries.

Voice of Youth Advocates

The bimonthly *Voice of Youth Advocates* (*VOYA*) should be your first step in acquainting yourself with what is new and important in teen literature and library service to teens. Because it focuses specifically on services for the twelve- to eighteen-year-old library patron, it can provide broader coverage of YA issues than can journals that must also cover children's or adults' books and services. Recurring columns on topics such as graphic novels, design of teen areas, technology, programming, and adult materials with teen appeal do an excellent job at examining the breadth of teen library service. Feature articles offer further in-depth information on topics of interest and importance to teens. Recent features have addressed body image, assigned summer reading lists, sex and sexuality in teen fiction, and the library's role as a safe place for teens.

Although the journal offers wonderful articles and columns, the majority of its pages are devoted to reviews. Due to its comprehensive rating system, *VOYA*'s reviews are especially helpful for the librarian who is new to working with YA literature. Each work is given a grade-level interest range (middle school, junior high, senior high, or adult market with teen appeal), which helps you to picture who the prospective readers would be as you read through the review. Additionally, each review gives independent quality

Figure 4-3 ● **How to Read Reviews**

1. **Familiarize yourself with the journal and its reviewing policy.** Does it review everything it receives? Does it print only favorable reviews? Is it intended for use in selecting books mainly for schools, for public libraries, or for the general public? Keep these standards in mind when reading a review as they may influence how and why a book is or is not recommended for purchase.

2. **Note the rating system and age recommendation, if any.** Many journals that focus on books for teens and children will suggest age ranges or grade levels. In such cases, it is necessary to know if 10–12 means tenth through twelfth grades or ten- to twelve-year-olds in order to accurately assess a book's place in your collection and what age group you might suggest the book to. Some journals will use codes to identify certain qualities, such as anticipated popularity, literary quality, or specific deficiencies. Knowing what the codes mean will allow you to skim through reviews that either do not apply to the age group you serve or do not have the quality you may need. Additionally, these codes will call your attention to those titles that merit an extra thorough read-through.

3. **Read the review for content.** What is the book about? Will teens in your community be interested in and relate to the plot? Was the plot described in an engaging way? Does the character sound interesting? Does the reviewer compare the book to other popular works or authors? Is another book mentioned as a preferred alternative? Also note mentions of challenging content, such as heavy drug use, casual sex, graphic violence, or rough language.

4. **Read the review for appeal.** What kind of adjectives does the reviewer use? Is the book about a typical adventure or a thrilling adventure? Terms like *spicy, mature, shocking,* or *edgy* tell you something about a book, as do words like *gentle, quiet, traditional,* or *cozy.* Note also descriptions that suggest crossover appeal, as, for example, characters in a fantasy novel who are described as being "angsty, urban Goths." The book may be wonderful and have well-described appeal factors, but consider *who* the book will appeal to. Can you imagine patrons who would be interested in reading such a book based on its appeal?

5. **Read between the lines.** Much can be learned from the tone of a review. Does the reviewer's excitement for the book jump off the page, or do you detect a sneer in the way the author relates the plotline? Unwritten impressions will rarely be crucial in terms of pitching a book to a patron, but they may suggest that you should take another look at a book before pitching it based on a review alone. At the same time, some reviews are so glowing across several journals that you can recommend the book practically without a second glance.

and popularity ratings. While it may be necessary to limit selection to those books that receive high marks in both categories, it is important to acknowledge the value of highly popular books, even if, according to reviews, they are not of very high quality. The availability of popular fiction and nonfiction for teen browsing will not only increase the library's cool factor but also help to establish the library as a location for teens to find the information that is important to them. This is a crucial step in ingraining in our next generation of taxpayers that the library is a valid and relevant establishment.

Booklist

If you are currently selecting materials for your library, you are most likely familiar with *Booklist*, published twenty times throughout the year. Books for youth are reviewed toward the back in the journal, after the adult fiction and nonfiction reviews and special interest sections. The "Books for Youth" section is broken into general age categories for older readers, middle readers, and the young. Librarians with a focus on high school readers will be most interested in the reviews of books for older readers, while those who work with readers in middle school and junior high school will find materials of use in the reviews of books for middle readers as well. *Booklist* includes only items that are recommended for purchase, but the extent of endorsement can, of course, vary. Starred reviews for all age ranges are separated from the general reviews and are not to be missed.

Also useful in *Booklist* are the adult titles recommended for teens, indicated by symbols and brief endorsements at the end of reviews in the general fiction and nonfiction sections. *Booklist* has done a great thing in acknowledging that many adult titles hold great teen appeal, but read the suggestions with a grain of salt. Paying close attention to exactly *why* these titles are recommended is very important. Is the narrative particularly compelling? Does the main character appear especially relatable to a teen? Or is this the niche book that will be the perfect match for that unique teen with a burning interest in the early days of the consumer flight industry?

One of *Booklist*'s strengths is the inclusion of spotlight features on a broad range of topics. If you find your collection lacking in multicultural fiction or want to bulk up on romance or historical fiction, these issues can be quite valuable. New titles and titles for youth are always included in the spotlight features as well. *Booklist* also offers a searchable database of its reviews, special highlighted lists, and feature articles. This online service should extend the usefulness and accessibility of *Booklist*'s features for readers' advisors.

School Library Journal

While *School Library Journal* (*SLJ*) contains many features that are of particular use and interest to school librarians, its usefulness extends beyond the school setting. In fact, it functions as the youth material and services counterpart to *Library Journal* and should not be missed by those intending to improve their knowledge of teen materials. Relevant reviews in *SLJ* are found in the "Fifth Grade and Up" section as well as in the "Adult Books for Teens" section that follows it. While all of the journals I have discussed review both nonfiction and fiction for teens, *SLJ* is often the most useful source of information about popular nonfiction for teens. Reviews of books on crafting, extreme sports, beauty, and self-help for teens can be frequently found in *SLJ*.

Reading *SLJ* in conjunction with *VOYA* and *Booklist* provides some interesting contrasts. It is not entirely uncommon to find vastly differing opinions about a book from journal to journal. The contrasts can be very useful and enlightening, especially when each review highlights the aspects that stood out to that particular reviewer. Sometimes, the contrasts are due to an aspect that is more or less absent from reviews of adult fiction books: morality. This is not to say that a review that comments on the morality of a character or her decisions is less objective or useful, but it does once again bring up the idea that books for teens should be good for them, but books for adults simply ought to be good. If you are reading journals as a selection tool, noting why a reviewer did not like a book can be very useful. Did the character not ring true, or did the character not make morally astute choices? Although a reviewer's perspective, or lack of perspective, on a character's morality should not be your only deciding factor, if the issue is raised in a review, you should give it some extra thought when considering prospective readers.

Conclusion

Becoming adequately acquainted with teen literature to be comfortable advising readers on what to choose is a long process, but every book read or skimmed and every review perused will steadily add to the bank of knowledge on which you can draw. Staying abreast of new titles and developments in teen literature, creating and moving forward with a reading plan, and staying attuned to appeal factors and commonalities within the books read will slowly but surely help to build familiarity and confidence. Anyone who has worked at a reference or information desk is familiar with the wonderful serendipity that occurs when our research into the answers to questions from our patrons opens our own eyes to new ideas. Both seeking out young adult literature to read and reading it create similar serendipitous opportunities—for finding out about teen culture, for uncovering interesting stories, and even for finding some potential new favorites. Being open and enthusiastic about these new experiences is one of the best ways we can serve teens; our enthusiasm, when visible to our teen patrons, welcomes and encourages their use of the library and their interest in reading.

Notes

1. J. K. Rowling, *Harry Potter and the Sorcerer's Stone* (New York: Arthur A. Levine Books, 1997).

2. Liesa Abrams, "Talkin' Teen," *Writers Digest* 85 (November 2005): 56–57.

3. http://www.ala.org/ala/yalsa/profdev/syllabiyoung.htm.

4. Diana Tixier Herald, *Teen Genreflecting: A Guide to Reading Interests* (Westport, CT: Libraries Unlimited, 2003). Patrick Jones, *A Core Collection for Young Adults* (New York: Neal-Schuman, 2003).

5. Adult Reading Round Table Steering Committee, "ARRT Young Adult Genre Fiction List" (Adult Reading Round Table of Illinois, 2002). Available for purchase through http://www.arrtreads.org or may be obtained through the subscription database NoveList.

6. Beatrice Sparks, ed., *Go Ask Alice* (Englewood Cliffs, NJ: Prentice-Hall, 1971).

Part Three

● ● ● ● ● ● ● ● ● ● ● ● ● ●

Taking Action

5 Opening the Readers' Advisory Interview

●

Now that we have considered the nature of YA literature and the general principles of readers' advisory service for teens, we will explore the elements that make a readers' advisory interaction with a teenager truly successful. While teens are unique, they are not mystical creatures who speak an entirely different language—it is only slightly different. A readers' advisory interview with a teen can be very rewarding for both of you, but to pave the way, you need to get the conversation off to a good start. To ensure the greatest success, you need to adapt the techniques for opening an interview with an adult to reflect the differing needs and perspectives of a teen.

This chapter will cover

- The general philosophy behind opening a readers' advisory interview
- How to modify readers' advisory techniques for teens
- Conversation starters that work
- Recognizing and respecting teens' needs for library resources (or what happens when your best efforts at readers' advisory for teens are shot down)

Talking to Strangers

Opening a readers' advisory (RA) interview is basically just starting a conversation—something librarians do every day. We may follow up on a reference interaction and call a patron whom we have never met in hopes of eliciting more information about her question. We may respond to an inquiry from a patron who comes to the desk looking for a book he cannot find. Or we may approach a person who appears to need help and end up giving an impromptu tour of the library. As adults, we have conversations with strangers daily—the clerk at the grocery store, the bank teller, the insurance agent on the telephone—and these other adults are typically just as used to talking with strangers. But when teens seek out help or information, the dynamic is often different. Long gone are the days of *ma'am* and *sir* in many parts of the country, but the construct behind the formalities remains: adults and teens hold different positions in our social structure. Teens may embrace these differences and apply them to their own social dealings as "Respect your elders," "Question authority," or some attitude in the vast middle ground. Each teen's perspective is going to be different, based on family culture, history, and personal preference. A librarian working with teens should be prepared for the wide variety. The teen who comfortably glides to the reference desk with the maturity and grace of an adult to chat about a good book and ask about a new one is rare (and wonderful), but just because many teens would not think to do that does not mean that they cannot participate in a productive RA interaction. The onus is on you, the librarian, the adult in the situation, to make sure that teens' reading needs are being met in your library. And the only way to find out is to ask.

That said, we cannot just walk up to teens and ask, "Excuse me, are your reading needs being met?" or we would be greeted with the raised-brow look that we are so familiar with—the one that says, "What are you, nuts?!" First and foremost in an interaction with teens is approachability. Patrick Jones, in *Connecting Young Adults and Libraries*, hits the nail on the head when he says that effective library services are

> a combination of skills, knowledge, and attitudes. The contention
> here is that YA work perhaps is different from other library work
> in that without the "right" attitude as a base, the other two traits
> [skills and knowledge] do not matter as much.[1]

If teens perceive that you are unhappy that they are in the area, uneasy suggesting books for them, or would rather be reading the journal in front of you, it will spoil your chances to have successful RA interactions. It does not matter how many sure bets you know, how up-to-date you are on the latest installment of the Gossip Girl series, or how proficiently you can search NoveList to get to a book that meets their interest. It is likely you will not get the chance to use any of these talents. Facial expressions and body language can go a long way. A warm smile and welcoming eye contact when teens enter your area or when you enter the teen area will help to demonstrate that you are receptive to interaction.

Take a Walk

When you think back to the last three libraries you entered, can you recall the location of the teen section in relation to the closest service desk? Most likely, unless the library had an entire teen department, complete with its own service desk, the teen area was a reasonable distance from the reference desk. Such a location allows teens a space that is out of heavy traffic patterns, is often a distance from dedicated quiet areas, and gives the impression that the librarian is not lurking behind the stacks with an eye out for misbehavior. These are great qualities that are crucial to well-used teen areas, but they can pose a logistical challenge to interacting with teens. Especially because of the setup of many libraries, it is very important for the librarian to leave the service desk and move into the stacks and teen browsing areas from time to time.

Oftentimes, we venture into the teen area when we suspect some kind of misbehavior—we hear laughter that seems too loud, a suspicious crash, or something of the like. It is important to monitor behavior. This is a completely valid activity. However, because we tend to leave teens to their own devices in a library until a behavior issue arises, it is imperative to be a positive, proactive presence as well if we hope to have positive interactions. One of our favorite strategies for being present for a good reason is filling displays in the area. Browsing the shelves to select books to display puts you in the same position as the teens—looking for a good book. This equalization of position—though your purposes may be different—can lead to conversations about the book you have in your hand or the book the teen next to you has in his hand, and may lead to a productive readers' advisory interaction (see fig. 5-1).

Another reason we often venture into the teen area is to help locate a book for a patron. I would strongly encourage this practice whenever it is

---

Figure 5-1 • Conversation Starters to Use while Browsing the Shelves
• •

If you just so happen to be looking for a book while a teen is browsing the shelves, turn the "coincidence" into an attempt at a readers' advisory interaction. Try using the following conversation starters:

1. Have you read this one? I've been hearing a lot of people talking about it.
2. I really enjoyed that one—did you know it's the second in a series?
3. I've never read anything by that author. Is he good?
4. I happened to notice you've got [name of book]. If you like that kind of book, [name of a similar book] is another good one.
5. Are you looking for a particular book that I could help you spot?
6. Looking for something for fun or for school?
7. If you don't find the one you're looking for, let me know—it might be on display or in a cart.

possible and practical to leave the desk, especially with teens. Walking with a teen to the shelves offers the opportunity for a few leading questions, such as, "How did you hear about this book?" or, "Are you doing a book report, or is it something for fun?" Sometimes these are key questions. Perhaps the patron got the title as a suggestion from a teacher or friend but really wants something vastly different, in which case you can guide her in the direction she prefers. Or perhaps the reader is voraciously devouring everything set in the Vietnam era and you can offer some additions to the reading list. Even if the book you set out to find is the exact (and only) one the teen wants, asking a question is a friendly gesture and helps to establish that you are there to help people actually find the books they want to read, not just to point them in the right direction.

After walking a teen to the shelf, we often will pull the book and ask if that is the desired title. It is not uncommon for someone to use the catalog to look up a title and end up with a book that has the same name but a different author. This presents a great opportunity to offer a tip on using the online public access catalog (OPAC) and assist the patron in getting the preferred work. If the patron has found the desired book, offering a comment about it or its author will indicate that you are open to YA literature and, you can hope, help the teen feel more comfortable asking questions. Figure 5-2 offers some suggestions for making small talk, but they come with two warnings. First, never lie about a book—if you have not read it, do not say you have. If you did not like it, do not say you did. Honesty in your interactions is a close second in importance to approachability with teen patrons. Second, sometimes patrons want the anonymity of a straightforward, business-like interaction. If you sense that the patron is resistant to engaging with you about discussing a book, or if the book is one that you know contains touchy

Figure 5-2 • Small Talk in the Stacks: What to Say about the Books You Help Patrons Find

1. I've been hearing a lot of buzz about this one—it sounds great.
2. She is one of my favorite authors. Have you read anything else by her?
3. If you like books with [action, good descriptions, really authentic settings, funny dialog], you might really like this.
4. This is one I've been meaning to read for a long time. Next time you're in you should let me know how you liked it.
5. The cover of this one always catches my eye when it's on display.

subjects, be sensitive and tailor your comments to what the patron needs. This requires a bit of mind reading, but paying attention to a patron's nonverbal cues and gauging your response accordingly is a step in the right direction.

Another way that venturing into the stacks functions as a great lead-in to a readers' advisory interview is that interactions breed more interactions. Just as the first raised hand elicits more raised hands in a classroom, helping one patron find the right book will very often lead to more patrons asking for help, or at least tossing a hopeful and welcoming glance in our direction. When teens see us happily engaging with other teens, helpfully answering their questions, and enthusiastically recommending books, we are involved in the best possible type of advertising. Frequently, we have observed that when we make a trip into the stacks to help a patron find the DVD she wants or the graphic novel that has eluded her, other teens take notice, and as soon as we part ways with the first patron, we are deluged with other requests. Once teens see someone that they can relate to, someone they recognize from school, or someone they might bump into at a sports event accepting help from a librarian, it is suddenly more acceptable for them to ask their own question.

Alternative Methods of Connecting

More and more, teens' lives happen online. Recently, I observed two teenage girls lounging on bean bags in our teen area with their cell phones, but they were not talking on their phones. They appeared to be sending text messages, an increasingly popular way of communicating. What I found even more interesting was when the girls, without any sound passing between them, looked up at each other and giggled. They had been texting one another. Even five years ago teens passed intricately folded paper notes back and forth between classes and behind teachers' backs or scribbled to one another on a notebook while trying to maintain the illusion of work in the library. Teens today are keeping in touch via technology. Cell phones, chat, and Internet boards like MySpace or Friendster have become a powerful communication force for teens. If libraries do not acknowledge that teens communicate and conduct much of their lives online, we will lose contact with them and be viewed as inaccessible. Keeping this in mind, consider providing readers' advisory services and contact information through your library's webpage and being accessible through instant messaging. To initiate readers' advisory conversations, being present in virtual teen hang-outs is just as important as physically entering the teen space in your library.

Once you have entered the stacks, put yourself in the position of the teens. If you smile, display an inviting attitude, and make an unobtrusive but clear offer of help and a teen responds positively, you will have surmounted one of the most difficult barriers to providing teen service. You will have gained an opening for conversation, the teen's attention, and a chance to fill a reading need. On the other hand, if you are the most welcoming, the most helpful, the most respectful and nonthreatening librarian you can be and no one responds, keep trying and do not despair. Sometimes a teen just wants to quietly browse the shelves, flip through a pile of magazines or CDs, or sit on the floor in front of the Inu Yasha books, reading one after another. Sometimes a teen needs some downtime away from prying eyes or helpful offers or boisterous friends. And sometimes a teen is embarking on a hunt that will take him to his new favorite book, a solo journey that can be one of the most empowering reading experiences possible. All of these endeavors are worthwhile and ought to be respected because they are serving a need the teen has at that particular time. As a result, even if you do not walk back to the desk with a flurry of hash marks to add to your statistics sheet, you have achieved an important outcome. A teen has found time to be in the library, and you have allowed him to do what he wants and needs to be doing. The materials selected, the space created, and the help offered all enable the teen to meet his immediate developmental and personal needs.

Note

1. Patrick Jones, *Connecting Young Adults and Libraries*, 2nd ed. (New York: Neal-Schuman, 1998), 180.

6
Detecting Interest

O nce we have opened the door to a readers' advisory interview with a teen patron, we must quickly and carefully begin the process of narrowing the field of potential book matches to the few that the patron might realistically be interested in. We do this by using the techniques for detecting interest and describing appeal that were briefly discussed in chapter 3. We can detect interest by asking the types of questions that will open the patron up to discussing more about the material he or she is looking for. When we are working with teens who may not be used to articulating their reading interests or are not familiar with commonly used terminology, we may need to adapt the typical readers' advisory interview techniques to their needs.

This chapter will examine techniques to use after successfully opening the interview that will aid in determining which books will be the best fit for your teen patron, including

- Questions to ask in order to detect a patron's interests
- Suggestions for eliciting information on taste and reading ability
- Methods to use to get a teen patron talking

Detecting Interest: Assignment or Not?

Much of teens' reading is directed by school assignments. Teens may be required to read a specific title, a book that meets certain criteria (length, historical time period, and the like), or a book of their own choosing, perhaps for a report or a sustained silent reading program. Knowing why a patron is looking for a book may influence your suggestions, especially if the book must meet a teacher's requirements. Chapter 8 explains how to help a patron find a book that is needed for an assignment and that meets specific requirements.

Four Little Questions and How They Work

A patron looking for something to read for fun or for an open reading assignment may have an idea of what she would like, or she may not. Regardless, some books will hit the mark while others will be completely wild throws. The only way to zero in on that perfect book is to seek out what the teen is interested in reading. This process, which has the potential to be time consuming, must happen fairly quickly in order to retain the patron's interest and to demonstrate that we have a plan for finding a book and are willing to do what it takes to help. Teens are busy people. Remember Ranganathan's law and do not waste their time, or yours. One way of accomplishing this is to quickly narrow the field before delving more deeply into specifics. The four conversation-opening questions presented in figure 6-1 will help teens articulate their reading interests.

Though the four questions may seem simplistic or repetitive, there is a rationale behind using one or more of them to start a readers' advisory interview with a teen. What information is obtained from these questions, and why is it useful?

1. Do you read a lot or not so much?

Asking teens if they read a lot accomplishes multiple goals. First, a teen's response to this question will frequently give you a sense of the teen's attitude about reading. Someone who replies, "Well, sort of, but mostly for school," may have a very different relationship with books and reading than the teen who answers, "Yeah. I read a lot, like a book a week. I read the last Harry Potter in two days!" or, "No, not really." Asking if a teen reads a lot will often lead to clues about reading level or proficiency as well. Pay close attention to what the teen says in response to this question. Enthusiastic readers will often go on to tell about the last great book they read, or the reading slump they have hit, or how they want two copies

Figure 6-1　●　Four Quick Questions for Determining Reading Interests

. . . .

1. Do you read a lot or not so much?

2. Are you looking for a specific book that you know of?

3. Can you think of a book that you've liked recently?

4. Have you read anything recently that you really hated?

of a book so that they can share with a friend. Finding out that such teens have read quite a bit of the new fiction on display or have recently finished a popular series will expedite the interaction because you will know which titles to skip over. It is also quite possible that the question will reveal teens who do not enjoy reading—either because they find it difficult or because they cannot seem to find materials of real interest. Such information can help you make suggestions that are at an appropriate reading level and may lead to alternative reading materials, such as browsable nonfiction, comics, magazines, and high-interest photo essay books. Additionally, it may provide an opportunity for you to highlight other areas of the collection that the teen may be interested in but not aware of, such as DVDs, computer software, or how-to books that may help the teen begin to identify the library as a source of information that is applicable to his or her life. Or it could just give you the extra drive to exhaust every avenue possible to find a great read for the patron.

When teens tell how much they read, it is important to be fully accepting of their responses. If a teen required to find a free-reading book says, "No, I don't read a lot. Reading is stupid," and you reply by extolling the joys of reading, you will find the once-opened door to conversation slammed in your face quicker than you can say, "Have you read *Stormbreaker*?"[1] A much more productive approach might be to empathize with the patron. Saying, "Well, if you need a book, we should at least try to find one that you won't be totally bored with," could do more to facilitate a positive interaction because finding a book that will not be too boring might be the most that the teen hopes for. Meeting her on her own terms, being empathetic about the task as she sees it, and offering help that goes beyond the minimum answers her need and may surpass her expectations. This is a conversation, not a lesson, and the job of the readers' advisor is to meet the need of the patron, wherever that patron happens to be along the reading spectrum.

2. Are you looking for a specific book that you know of?

This seems to be a straightforward and simple question with a straightforward and simple answer. Sometimes it is. But frequently teens come to the desk with a book in mind . . . or almost in mind. They may be looking for a book that they saw someone reading in school, but they did not catch the whole title. Or they may be hoping that there is a new installment in their favorite series. Frequently, they have already looked for a book that they read about online but were unable to find. Because our local bookstore, which is right around the corner, frequently gets titles in stock and out on display faster than ours can be cataloged—or even ordered in some cases—we have received several great suggestions for purchase from teens who come in looking for something they saw in the bookstore window display. Asking teens if they have something specific in mind may also prompt them to reply with something like, "I finished the last Cirque du Freak[2] book last week. Is the new one out yet?" which can lead to finding the book, placing a hold on something not yet released, guiding the patron to a list of recommended vampire books, or locating an acceptable in-the-meantime title to tide him over. Asking patrons if they are looking for a specific book gives them the opportunity to get your help in finding something they may have thought unavailable, or it may offer a great jumping-off point for other new book suggestions.

3. Can you think of a book that you've liked recently?

We have found that asking about a recently enjoyed book can be one of the most revealing questions—as long as we follow up with the right questions afterward. Sometimes it is an unnecessary question in that teens may give the same response that they gave to the second question. But asking about a recently enjoyed book gives at least two types of information. From the response, you may be able to gauge how recently a teen has read a book for fun and get a sense of the types of material and reading level he is interested in. It is not uncommon for the last good book to be something that appears to be far below the typical reading level for the patron's grade. If the patron is fourteen years old but mentions the Dear America series of historical diaries, it could very well indicate the reading level that the patron is comfortable with. It could also be that those books just happened to be the last ones that really made a lasting impression on the reader—or they could be old favorites that the patron revisits from time to time because they are safe and familiar. Clarifying questions are crucial in a situation like this in order to suggest a book that neither insults the teen with its simplicity nor overwhelms her with its complexity. Some useful follow-up questions are presented in figure 6-2.

In addition to providing hints about a patron's reading level, the follow-up questions are important because the last book enjoyed is not always typical of the patron's usual interest. The Harry Potter series is the best and most common example. Many teens will reply that they liked the last Harry Potter but would not be interested in reading other fantasy novels. Sometimes a teen will have enjoyed a book assigned for school, like J. D. Salinger's *Catcher in the Rye*, but is not really looking for another classic. Getting to the crux of a book's appeal is crucial to finding good suggestions for further reading.

Figure 6-2 ● Follow-Up Questions to Glean More Insight from a Teen's Last Favorite Book

. . . .

1. Have you read other books like that? (Offer examples of titles in the same genre.)
2. Do you think you'd like to read another book about (a particular time period/wizards/family issues/Africa) or with a character who (has magical powers/is physically disabled/is like someone you might know)?
3. Did you read that book recently? Can you tell me what you remember liking about it?
4. Was that something that you read for school, or was it for fun?

Someone who loved the detailed descriptions and rich setting of Harry Potter is looking for a different reading experience than the reader who latched on to Harry's inner quest for the truth and constant battle against evil. A reader who relished the idea of reading a banned book like *Catcher* and identified with Holden's loner status would be happy with a different book than the reader who focused on the question of Holden's decreasing grasp on reality. Often, when a book's appeal can be as multifaceted as that of *Catcher in the Rye*, simply asking the teen to tell you about the book will yield more insight than carefully phrased questions. If the book really is a favorite, the teen should have some feelings about it. Broadly phrased, open-ended questions allow the teen to share some of those feelings. If this approach seems more involved than the teen is interested in, naming specific elements and offering them as options for further reading is a good way to get at the same information. Saying, "Was it the New York setting, or the psychological stuff Holden was going through, or the whole controversy surrounding the book that you remember liking the most?" This gives the teen the opportunity to choose one of the options or to say, "Actually, I thought it was cool how concerned he was with his little sister."

Clarifying questions are useful in understanding exactly what appeals to a teen. Elements such as humor are very subjective. When the teen wants a funny book, is he looking for slapstick humor, dark humor, or subtly tongue-in-cheek humor? Using examples or relating the type of humor to other media, like movies or TV shows, may be useful. Do not be surprised if the nature of a teen's interest is not entirely clear regarding more controversial topics. A repeat teen patron of ours asked for "provocative" books. Anything provocative would do. But she clearly had her own definition of *provocative*, because books dealing with political issues or hot-button social concerns always remained on the table when she left. When I finally had an opportunity to discuss her interests with her, it became clear that to her, *provocative* meant "sexy" or "spicy." We use words like this, words that have complex meanings that could be interpreted in a variety of ways, constantly. Expect teens to use them too, often with complexity and carefully veiled meanings. Granted, some topics may cause discomfort, either for the teen or for the librarian. That situation will be discussed in chapter 7.

4. Have you read anything recently that you really hated?

This is the question that often elicits the strongest response from teens. If the first three questions did not get the teen talking, chances are that this one will. As readers' advisors, we avoid bashing a book that might be a great work, but being open as a teen laments the tedium of John Steinbeck's *The Grapes of Wrath* or how Shakespeare is just stupid thrusts what may have been a lopsided conversation into the realm of books. If a teen says that she hated reading *Romeo and Juliet*, you can draw out her reading interests by using information about the book. Offering points about which the teen can become passionate helps focus her attention on what it was about the book, rather than about the reading experience itself, that she disliked. Saying, "So you're not into the classics?" or "I take it you don't like poetry?" will often nudge a teen in the direction of expressing what she *wished* the reading experience could have been like. If she disliked that the first lines of the play reveal that the young lovers die in the end, ask if it was the tragedy aspect or knowing what was going to happen that she did not like. Maybe a book with a tragic ending would be acceptable if the ending could not be anticipated throughout the story. The reader might also prefer a book with unexpected twists and turns that cannot be foreseen at the start of the story. Or perhaps the reader wants a love story with a happy ending.

Then again, the teen's main objection could be that she did not enjoy reading a historical work with difficult language and cultural references. Even this gives us something to work with. In this situation, offering to help the teen find something really new with "regular people," or perhaps even a book set locally, acknowledges that not all reading has to be historical and distant—it can be contemporary, futuristic, and even take place around the corner. If this question and the previous one do not yield enough useful information, it may help to prompt the patron. Being aware of commonly assigned books in the local schools really becomes useful here. Asking if the patron has read one of these books and how she liked it will sometimes get her talking about her likes and dislikes.

Asking about a book that the patron did not like might seem like a negative way of approaching the interaction, as if the reading experience is expected to be boring or lame. In fact, quite the opposite is true. If a teen can recall with fervor the last book he despised, chances are he will carry that experience with him for a while. Understanding what struck such a nerve, confronting that, and attempting to find a book that the teen will find appealing can turn a bad experience into a good one. By confronting the negative baggage that a reader may be carrying around, we acknowledge that we take his views seriously and that we will try to do better in the future. Recall that unlike adult readers, most young readers are assigned the bulk of their reading material—it is not self-selected. If a teen is taking the giant step of asking for help in finding a book, it is crucial to convey the idea that our job as readers' advisors is to find the book that the teen *wants* to read.

Delving Deeper

After a patron starts to articulate his or her needs and interests by responding to the top four questions, it is time to move on to more specific questions about standard appeal factors. As discussed in chapter 3, appeal factors are the elements that make up the overall feel and experience of the book. Not every appeal factor matters to every reader, but the elements that will make a difference in most readers' experience are character, story line, frame, and pacing. *Character* refers not only to who the characters are but also to how they are described and their roles in the story. *Story line*, clearly, describes what happens in the book. we have found that in the beginning phases of the readers' advisory process the plot of a book matters more to teens than it does to adults. The *frame* comprises all the elements that surround the story, such as setting, background, and subplots. *Pacing* refers to how quickly or slowly a story unfolds and moves to its conclusion.

Delving deeper into our patrons' interests requires that we ask specific questions about what they hope the reading experience will be like. Because teen readers may have a shorter personal reading history than adults, they may be unsure of how to answer the questions that we ask of adults when we assume they know about subgenres and literary qualities. Framing our questions with opposing options is a good way to address this issue. Rather than asking a teen, "What kind of fantasy do you like?" we can offer options: "Do you like fantasy that's more historical, such as medieval, or do you like more of a contemporary, urban setting?" The same can be done for more general qualities: "Are you looking for a book that's more about people and their relationships, or more about the actions of the main characters?"

"Do you want something that'll give you ideas to think about or talk about, or do you prefer a light, fun read that you don't have to think too hard about?" By naming specific options, we acknowledge that either choice is valid, which is especially important when working with teens.

Questions about Character

When asking questions about a reader's preferences in characters, we have two goals: to find out if the type of character is important to the teen's reading experience and to determine how the reader prefers the character to interact with the story. Does the patron want a character she can identify with as if she were a friend? Would the reader prefer to learn about someone very different from the people he knows? Does the age of the character matter? Should the character be an observer or an active agent in the story? Should the character think deeply about the activities and ideas in the book, or is action more important than introspection? Should the character interact with many other characters, just a few, or mostly within his or her internal world? Some questions to ask about character are presented in figure 6-3.

Questions about Story Line

As mentioned, teens tend to weigh story line more heavily in their decision to read a book than do many adults. Because of this, a readers' advisor must detect what elements are important for a teen patron's enjoyment of a story. Some teens enjoy the familiarity and predictability of plots that are repeated over and over again, as in series fiction. Others prefer each reading experience to present a new set of circumstances and events. For many teens, the inclusion of a particular ingredient in the story

---

Figure 6-3 ● Questions to Ask about Character

1. Do you like to read about the kind of people you know?
2. Is it OK if the characters are younger/older than you?
3. Would you rather read about regular people or extraordinary people, like wizards or movie stars or the rich and famous?
4. Do you want a book about a guy or a girl, or doesn't it matter?
5. Do you like a book that tells stories about a lot of different people, or is it better when a book mostly focuses on one person?

line is important—a happy ending, for example, or the presence of friendship. Many teens will approach the desk looking for a book with a specific plot element, such as abuse, death, adventure, or romance. They may also express a preferred story line through comparison to another book—for instance, asking for a book with an evil genius who cons characters from the fairy world as in Eoin Colfer's *Artemis Fowl*. When this happens, it is crucial to find out if it really was the plot that the reader liked or if it was the way in which various elements unrelated to plot (a child prodigy, clever humor, and supernatural overtones) coalesced into the total effect (which is most easily articulated by describing the plot) that contributed to the reader's enjoyment. Useful questions for detecting preferred story lines are presented in figure 6-4.

Questions about Frame

Frame is a term that few teens know in relation to books but that most teens understand in relation to their pleasure reading. What makes a book great? An entire imaginary landscape with its own traditions and lore? A gritty urban setting ripped from the headlines of this morning's paper? The lush description of the sights, smells, and sounds of Victorian England? Is a book better if you learn something about beekeeping, or car repair, or tracking polar bears? Frame can be difficult to describe, especially to a teen, but asking specific questions about features that a teen finds enjoyable or distracting while reading is a good way to approach it (see fig. 6-5).

Questions about Pacing

Accurately describing the pacing of a book is crucial when presenting a book to teens. All trust will be lost if the book we describe as "so exciting that you can't put it down" crawls along at a snail's

---

Figure 6-4 ● **Questions to Ask about Story Line**
. . . .

1. Are you more interested in the people or the action in a book?

2. Do you want something that's just a fun read, or something more about issues and ideas?

3. Are you bothered by strong language/violent scenes/sexy scenes or the like?

4. Do you like books that present the perspectives of a few different people? Such as when each chapter is narrated by a different character or presents a different person's point of view?

Figure 6-5 ● Questions to Ask about Frame

· ·

1. Do you read fantasy books?
2. What about sci-fi, stories in futuristic settings?
3. Do you like books set in the past? Any particular time period?
4. Does detail bog you down when you read, or do you like it?
5. Are you interested in any sports or hobbies that you think you might like to read about in a novel?
6. Have you read books that are written like a diary or letters? Do you like those?

Figure 6-6 ● Questions to Ask about Pacing

· ·

1. Are you looking for a book with action that moves quickly or for something a little slower?
2. Do you like books with a lot of dialogue, lots of conversations between the characters?
3. Is it important to know what the characters are thinking about, or would you rather have characters that just dive into action?
4. Do you mind if it takes a few chapters to get into the action of the story?

---

pace until its last quarter. Nor will a teen be satisfied if he is looking for something to last him through a week-long summer vacation with his family and you suggest a book that whips through its story at breakneck speed. Determining the right pace for a book is not just about how quickly it can be read but also about how much time the reader wants to spend and how deeply the reader wants to connect with the story. Questions that will help you make decisions about pacing are presented in figure 6-6.

A Word on Determining Reading Level

If the previous questions do not help you clearly identify a patron's comfortable reading level—in terms of both reading ability and maturity level—it can be helpful to ask a few more questions to steer your book suggestions. A teen's physical appearance can be misleading at times. Girls who hit puberty early and enjoy wearing makeup and adult clothing styles or boys who have developed deep voices or athletic, muscular builds are not always as emotionally or academically mature as they look. Likewise, based on physical development and demeanor, it is not uncommon to assume that teenagers are much younger than they actually are. Determining a patron's reading level tends to be particular to working with young people, and while reading level can be a useful clue to possible interests, it is more a factor to consider than an appeal factor to match. Just because a patron read one complexly written literary novel does not mean he would be comfortable or interested in reading another. Conversely, if a high school junior's all-time-favorite book is Gary Paulsen's *Hatchet*, there is no reason to assume that all suggested books must be written at a middle school reading level. Sometimes a teen wants to challenge herself by reading something beyond her usual fare. Sometimes she wants a comfortable book that allows a fluid reading experience. Determining reading level is especially important when working with the lower and upper ends of the young adult spectrum. A twelve-year-old may ask a question at the adult reference/readers' advisory desk regardless of whether he wants to read something from the children's department, the teen department, or a dense Victorian novel. Readers' advisors commonly react to older teens' reading requests by nudging them into the adult fiction section, but they may be perfectly happy reading teen fiction. The only way to know is to ask. Some useful questions for assessing reading level can be found in figure 6-7.

With older teens, asking flat out if they read young adult fiction is the easiest and least ambiguous way to determine whether or not they are open to these books (some are not and prefer books published for the adult market). With younger teens, it is often easier to inquire about book length and density than to ask if they read young adult or children's books. The rationale behind the different approaches is twofold. First, older teens with more

---

Figure 6-7 • **Questions to Ask When Trying to Determine Reading Level**

1. Do you read a lot?
2. Are you looking for something quick, or do you want to spend a little more time getting into the book?
3. What grade are you in?
4. Would something like this [with suggested book in hand] be more book than you want today?
5. Do you mind books that are kind of dense—for example, books that have lots of description?

autonomy are more likely to be familiar with the term *young adult fiction* due to their experience as consumers browsing in bookstores and seeking out titles online. Second, younger readers, although they usually understand that the teen area has different books from the children's or adults' departments, move back and forth between the sections with greater ease than we may realize, and therefore do not specifically identify their reading as "children's" or "young adult" because it is all *their* reading.

Conclusion

Your teen patrons looking for books can run the gamut from exuberant readers, still on a high from the last book they read, who can tell you just what they liked and just what they want to read about next to reserved teens unsure of how they feel about books and reading and uncertain about what they are looking for. Detecting interest can be a frustrating or an energizing phase of the readers' advisory process, but as long as you are able to extract a few key details that you can apply to the search for a good book, the experience will be successful. Listening carefully to the answers teens give us and asking clarifying questions when necessary will aid our search for the teens' real interests. Building on the answers we receive by asking more related questions will help to detect nuances in the teens' interests too. In the next chapter, we will examine what amounts to the opposite of this phase: articulating the appeal of the book. Thinking about how we can articulate the appeal of books to teens is a good exercise in putting ourselves in the shoes of the teens we hope will express their reading interests to us.

Notes

1. Anthony Horowitz, *Stormbreaker* (New York: Philomel Books, 2001).
2. Darren Shan, *Cirque du Freak: The Saga of Darren Shan* (Boston: Little, Brown, 2001).

7. Articulating Appeal

The glamour moment of any readers' advisory interaction is the actual book pitch that is made to the patron. Here is the phase where all of our efforts begin to coalesce and culminate, we hope, in getting a book into the teen's hand. This moment is the one during which we hope another teen (or maybe our supervisor) will walk by and see just how effective and approachable we are. If you still have a teen's ear at this point, the big work has been done. If you are able to clearly articulate to the teen why the books you are suggesting may be fun and interesting reads, you will have smooth sailing from here on out. However, pitching the book (or booktalking it, or articulating its appeal) in a way that makes it sound like the perfect book for that teen at that time involves deliberate forethought and careful wording. How do you say "It's great" in just the right way? Especially if the book you are suggesting is one that you are unfamiliar with—or worse yet, your all-time favorite—finding the correct words can be difficult. Here is the make-or-break opportunity to help a teen find a book.

This chapter will consider

- Using language and jargon in a teen-friendly manner
- Adapting book descriptions into appeal-based pitches
- Effectively discussing sensitive issues in a book pitch
- Facing and working through challenges to suggested books

The Perfect Word Is Not Always the Perfect Word

We librarians love our lingo. We have acronyms and fancy words for every type of writing and appeal factor possible. This helps us to clearly articulate exactly what the experience of reading a book is like, but when working with teens, it is crucial to keep our vocabulary in mind. Does "a compelling and tightly woven coming-of-age saga" sound like something that a teen would be interested in? Would any given teen on the street even know what you mean? Do not forgo the lingo, just be mindful of how it is used. If a book is "complex and multilayered," what about telling the teen, "It's a complex story. A lot of different characters' stories are all going on at the same time, but then the layers all slowly come together and you get the whole picture by the end." Dumbing down our language does not work because teens are experts at picking up condescension. What does work is using language carefully and adding clarification for more esoteric terms. Even very common readers' advisory terminology can be clarified without making a teen feel talked down to. For example, "It's a real page-turner. The story starts out with a bang and it just pulls you through. It's one of those books that's hard to put down." Here, a term is introduced (a real page-turner), explained (starts out with a bang, pulls you through), and put into a concrete description of how it feels to read a book with this characteristic (hard to put down). When we clarify our terminology within the context of its use, we introduce teens to terms that they will encounter again and again in the world of books. Because working with teens will inherently include some instruction on getting the most out of the library, this way of describing books dovetails nicely with both the educational component of library work with teens and the pure enjoyment of reading.

Paying close attention to the words that our teen patrons use is equally important. If a teen asks for a romance or a mystery or something scary, clarify what those terms mean to that individual. Recently, a teen came to the desk looking for a romance, but none of the books that fit the typical profile of a romance novel interested her. It was not until we asked some clarifying questions that we discovered that this teen wanted a tragic story of love gone bad—more like what would be considered a problem novel. She was not wrong in calling the book a romance, because that was the element she most identified with. It is all a matter of really and truly hearing what a teen is asking for.

The Pitch

When you feel that you have used the techniques in chapter 6 to gather enough information about the type of book your patron wants, repeat the facts that you have gleaned. This goes back to the active listening and good reference behaviors that we are familiar with. It is important to recall that although conversations for teen readers' advisory may be loosely structured and informal, the desired result is to give patrons what they want—so be sure to clarify before lunging for the shelves to pull out titles you hope will be matches. Saying something as simple as, "So it sounds as if you're looking for something fun and light for vacation?" or "I think we can find a really suspenseful mystery for you with vampires or something supernatural—does that sound good?" will demonstrate that you have been paying attention to your patron's responses and is that last check to be sure you understand what the patron meant. Your hope is that the patron either will validate your assessment so that you can move on to summarizing and suggesting books or will correct any erroneous assumptions you may have made so that you do not go off on the wrong track.

Plot and characters tend to be the most important elements to most teen readers, but if the readers' advisory interview reveals that another element is more important to a particular patron, be sure to include it as well. If the patron expresses interest in a specific type of character or pacing, adapt your pitch to address these components. Give the patron this information quickly and concisely and pay attention to his reaction. Does it appear that he is interested and wants more details, or is his lip curling as if you have offered him a dead rat? Elaborate if it appears that you have piqued his interest, but do not belabor the description of a book that the patron has already decided he does not want to read, unless you feel that your first description did not do justice to the true experience of reading the book.

Everyone makes snap judgments based on first impressions, and yes, we do judge books by their covers and titles. Since the quality of cover art varies greatly, sometimes great books get saddled with covers that give a misleading impression of their contents. Older titles, while still great and timely reads, will often be passed over if they have that genuine 1980s feel, conveyed by head-banded, big-haired teens wearing stonewashed jeans and sitting casually on porch steps. If you (bravely) choose to pitch an older book without an updated cover, or with a title that sounds goofy at first but may be supremely appropriate within the context of the story, acknowledge the lack of cool factor.

Formulating Your Pitch

Since we need to slightly adapt the way we talk to teens about recreational reading, we need to slightly adapt the format of our pitch as well. The main questions we need to address when pitching a book to teens are, What kind of book is it? Who is it about? What does this person do—what is the action? Which of the teen's needs or interests will the book serve? What is a benchmark for comparison? The Mad-Lib-style format in figure 7-1, which is adapted from Neal Wyatt's book *The Readers' Advisory*

Figure 7-1   ●   Fill-in-the-Blank Format for Articulating Appeal to Teens

It is a ___ book about a ___ who ___. If you like books that ___, you might like this one. People who have liked ___ have also liked this one.

Guide to Nonfiction, can help you to succinctly answer these questions.[1] Try using this format to identify the appeal of a book that you know well—and then try using the same book to identify appeal elements from a different reader's perspective.

The blanks can be completed in a variety of ways to emphasize different appeal elements for readers with different interests. Below are several ways to describe Markus Zusak's 2006 Printz Honor book, *I Am the Messenger:*

General Description
It is an interesting book about a do-nothing kind of guy who drives a cab and ends up getting sent on missions to deliver messages (that are sometimes pretty dangerous) by a mysterious stranger. If you like books with lots of twists, you might like this one. People who have liked mysteries and books by Chris Crutcher have liked this one.

For Someone Looking for a Mystery
It is a suspenseful book about an underage cab driver whose life gets turned upside down when he intervenes in a bank robbery, then gets tapped by a mysterious stranger to deliver messages to all kinds of people. If you like books that feature a character who has puzzles to solve and is sometimes in danger, you might like this one. People who have liked books that keep readers guessing until the end have liked this one.

For a Reader Most Interested in Characters
It is an Australian book about a guy who lives with his stinky dog and is not really doing anything with his life but driving a cab and playing poker with his buddies until he gets pushed into a complex situation where he ends up changing people's lives. If you like books that slowly reveal the main character's past and what goes on inside his head, and that introduce a bunch of interesting minor characters, you might like this one. People who have liked Rob Thomas's *Rats Saw God* and other books in which everything comes together at the end have liked this one.

While the emphasis in each pitch is different, nothing in any of them is deceitful or plays up elements that are not significant. Such adaptations will not be possible for all books simply because not every book will appeal to several types of readers. Never lie or exaggerate to make an element sound better than it actually is. If you find that you cannot create a character-focused description for a particular book, chances are that the title will not appeal to a character-focused reader—and it should not have to. Move on to another book and try again. Playing around with this format and applying it to different books will help you to answer the questions mentioned above so that you will have more ready matches when it is time to suggest a book to a reader. If this is a format that works for you, jot down notes for possible pitches in your logbook or reading file for each book that you read. This may help you to recall appealing elements more readily when pressed into action. Obviously, this is not the only way to describe books to teenagers. If the format feels awkward or unnatural to you, use any format you like as long as it answers the main questions listed above.

Sometimes it may take several tries before the book we pull off the shelf and pitch to a teen results in a match. If it appears that you have more misses than hits, ask the teen if any of the titles sound close to what she was looking for or allow her a chance to reformulate her request. It is also possible that the books you suggest sound thrilling and wonderful to a teen—but you would never know it from the look on her face. A strategy that often works when this happens is to pull and pitch several titles, then leave them where the teen can pick them up on her own, away from the watchful eyes of librarians, peers, or parents. Whether you stack them at the end of the bookshelf or place them on a nearby table, leaving the books accessible for browsing allows the teen the option to pick them up or pass them by. This technique is especially useful when suggesting books that have controversial content or sensitive subject matter. It takes pressure off the teen and allows her to choose whether to pick up a book, read a page or so, pass it by, or grab it and start reading immediately. If you employ this technique, it is important to remind the teen that if none of the books on the table look good to her or are not quite right, she is welcome to ask for follow-up help. Our line—always said with a smile—is, "Let me know if none of these work and I'll try again." This reinforces the idea that the reading choice is up to the teen and that finding the match is *our* job. Teens should not feel obligated to settle for something that sort of sounds OK just because we did not find a book they really wanted on the first try. We will try and try until we have found the right book.

Dealing with Sensitive Issues

As mentioned in chapter 2, some of the appeal teens find in reading may come when their ideas and personal boundaries are challenged in the relatively low-risk environment of a book. This, coupled with the varying stages of maturity and development among teens, has the potential to create tension either as teens seek out sensitive material or as we suggest books that meet a teen's interests and also contain potentially difficult elements. Touchy subjects always have been and always will be a part of the teen canon because the teenage years are all about discovering oneself in relation to peers, family, and the larger world. Whether this self-discovery happens through quiet contemplation, sexual experimentation, religious exploration, or challenging boundaries by acting out, trying to find the answers to the big questions enters most teens' minds and many teens' reading. Anyone working with teens and their reading interests should be prepared to present books with controversial elements without judgment or pressure in either direction.

What Are Sensitive Issues?

We never know what another reader's hot-button issues are, and this is both daunting and comforting. There is some content we can anticipate that the average patron may want to know about—such as graphic violence or explicit sex—but there are many other matters that may strike a nerve as a patron reads that we will never know about. Most people have their own boundaries when it comes to various issues. Some are completely unfazed by coarse language but cannot bear the thought of animals being harmed. Others do not mind allusions to sex or physical intimacy, but feel that detailed descriptions cross the line. Sometimes, though, the boundaries are more nebulous and the issues may be harder to pin down. For some readers, anything to do with current politics is a turn-off, or a book that deals with the death of a family member will hit too close for comfort, or a book in which a character endures bullying will mirror a recent and painful experience. It would be impossible to screen each title and warn each patron about every possibly sensitive issue. The best we can do is to be aware when issues, situations, or elements stand out in the titles we suggest and present these to the patron just as we would other elements: described in terms of how they add to the story or noted as features that some readers may be drawn to.

Often, librarians may be cautious about recommending a book that they know, for example, contains rough language or describes abuse because they are unsure if it would be "appropriate" for a patron at that age. This is a valid concern. However, because readers' advisory for teens focuses mainly on recreational reading, we can simply present a book and empower a teen to decide whether to read it or to choose a different title. This is a time when placing the books we suggest on a table or the end of a shelf is an effective tool. We can explain that the characters are interesting and funny and that the dialogue includes lots of cursing and then put the book down. After we leave, the patron can then make the decision to read it or not—and avoid being watched while choosing a book with sensitive content.

How Do Teens Feel about These Issues?

Much has been written and discussed lately about the sad state of teen literature—it promotes poor morals, it is full of smut and commercialism, it is all gloom and doom. It is true that one can find books written specifically for teens that include all of these elements and more. The critics imply that teens do not really want to be reading such books and that writers and publishers are foisting mature subject matter on children before they are ready. While some of this may be true for certain authors, publishers, or readers, our typical teen reader is very similar to our typical adult reader when it comes to sensitive subject matter. Some are drawn to it, some find solace or connection in reading it, and some prefer to avoid it. Because we will rarely know how the reader in front of us feels about sensitive issues, it is sometimes necessary to tread cautiously. This is especially true if we have that perfect book in mind that meets all of a patron's other interests but contains something that might be uncomfortable. Frequently, we can simply include the potentially difficult element in the description formula from chapter 6, using terms that a teen will pick up on, like *gritty*, *rough*, *racy*, *mature*, *heavy*, *violent*, or *in-your-face*. Or we can directly ask the teen if a sensitive element seems appropriate. "Does violence bother you?" is a good question to ask when helping teens find scary books, mysteries, or thrillers. Once we know what level of violence a teen is comfortable with, we can point our suggestions in that direction. Most often, though, we can simply say, "There's some sex in this one," or "This author writes from a Christian perspective," or "This one has a strong environmental message." Avoiding terms that suggest condemnation or endorsement but simply stating the facts is the key to suggesting these books, especially when we are unaware of how a teen feels about their content.

When teens specifically request a book about or containing a sensitive subject, it is important to respect their interest and try to meet their needs as best as possible. In readers' advisory for recreational reading, it is our job to direct teens to the books that we feel are appropriate based on their interests and reading level—not on our own judgment of what is "right" for someone that age to read about or know about. We do not know why the request is being made. If a teen asks for a fiction book about date rape, she could need it as background material for a report. She may want to read it to better understand the discussions surrounding a news story in the public eye. She may simply be interested in reading dramatic stories about people in difficult situations. Or she may want a book about date rape because it is something she or someone close to her has gone through. We do not always need to know why teens want a book; we just need to be sure they get the information and reading experience that they came to the library looking for.

Sometimes, though, a very young reader may come to our desk requesting a topic or title that seems far outside the typical reading range for someone his age. If this happens, treat the request just as you would any other: "Is it Judy Blume's *Forever* that you're looking for? The one about the girl in high school who falls in love?" It is possible that a young fan of *Superfudge* is just trying to get his hands on everything by his new favorite author and does not really want her more mature work detailing a first sexual experience. Or maybe he does. Mentioning a few of the appeal factors should help him decide quickly. When an eight-year-old comes to the adult desk looking for something by Stephen King, or "really scary stories," it could be that Stephen King is what his older brother is reading. Usually, the best course of action is to show the young reader the size of a Stephen King book, describe the plot, and suggest that there are many more books of scary stories you could help him find if he wants a few more to choose from.

Challenges, Formal and Informal

Sometimes, despite our best efforts to articulate the appeal of a book in a way that prepares a reader for its content, a mismatch occurs and a teen patron checks something out that either he is not comfortable with or his parents are not comfortable having him read. When this happens, it is possible that the librarian will face a challenge to the material, its location in the library, or the reasons it was handed to a particular teen. Anyone who does readers' advisory for teens on a regular basis will more likely than not have at least one encounter in which her judgment is called into question. Most of the time, a book challenge can be resolved between the librarian and the parent without escalation to a formal complaint or request for reconsideration of material. Usually, a parent's complaint about material that his or her child has been given is based on content that is more mature than the parent wishes the child to read. Just as we can never predict which issues will be especially sensitive to our teen readers, we cannot always predict which books will have content that parents will view as inappropriate.

Respond with Empathy

While our first reaction when confronted with a challenge may be to defend our selection, it is crucial at this stage to listen to the complainant. Often, a potentially volatile situation can be defused by being open to what the parents have to say and expressing empathy for their concern. Acknowledge that they are the ones who can best define what is acceptable in their home, and emphasize that you appreciate their interest in their children's reading material. You need not agree with the parents' assessment of the book, but you can certainly accept their feelings about what their teen has read. Saying, "I'm sorry this book upset you/your child," and offering help in finding another book that the parents approve of may be enough in some cases. This is the best-case scenario—the patron is appeased, you have maintained high-quality service by locating an alternative book, and the parents leave knowing that the library is a place that can be looked to for guidance in selecting materials for teens.

Offer Alternatives

It is important to offer alternative titles that address both the interests of the teen and the sensibilities of the parents. If the parents are amenable to working with you, ask them to describe the type of book they would like their child to read and what specifically bothered them about the book in question. This may illuminate issues to seek out or avoid. Proceed as you would with any other readers' advisory interaction, remaining sensitive to the needs of the patron. Because the parents may be happier and more comfortable if another librarian assists them in finding a new book, offer them that option as well. If no other librarians are available to assist these patrons, it may be helpful to suggest that someone could compile a list and call the parents. Providing lists of books or pointing the parents to reference sources that will help them seek out an appropriate title is a way to empower the parents to help their child on their own.

Dealing with Escalation

Of course, there are times when a parent or community member is not just concerned about the appropriateness of a book for one particular teen but feels that no teen (or adult, for that matter) should have access to the book. If the complainant is not appeased by an apology and alternatives to the initial suggestion, he may choose to file a formal complaint or request for reconsideration. At this point, the situation has typically escalated beyond what one librarian can or should be dealing with alone. Filing a formal complaint allows the patron to voice specific concerns to a larger audience, and usually moves the issue beyond the lone librarian to a group or committee that will share the burden of managing the complaint.

Sometimes, the complaint has to do with the book's placement in the teen collection. For this reason, having a solid and up-to-date collection development policy in place is essential. Ideally, this is a policy approved by the library director and board. If parents want to know why a particular book is cataloged for teens instead of for adults, explaining why the book conforms with the collection development policy or the guidelines for purchase of teen materials may help them to understand how the collection is designed to serve a diverse range of ages and interests.

Many excellent resources to aid librarians in dealing with challenges are available through the ALA's Office of Intellectual Freedom and other organizations, such as the National Coalition against Censorship. Being calm, organized, and prepared with research and reviews of the book in question are good starts at defending a challenge. Remember that you are not alone in having to defend the selection of a book or the recommendation of it to a teen. Asking for help and support from colleagues is a way not only to remain connected to a sympathetic community but also to gain more knowledge about the challenge process and the resources that can help to defend against a challenge.

Fall Down Seven Times, Get Up Eight

Effective readers' advisory is a skill. Effective readers' advisory for teens is a subset of this skill with its own unique set of challenges and techniques. Like any skill, mastery comes only with practice, and even after we have mastered the skills, we must constantly refresh our knowledge of the changing landscape of teen literature in order to provide the highest quality service to our young patrons. Staying in tune with teens takes effort. Try to work in public areas after school hours to maximize the likelihood of interacting with teens. Take chances by approaching teens in the stacks and asking them questions about the books they are seeking out. Try suggesting some books—and reassure the teens that it is OK if they do not like the titles. Practice formulating pitches for the books you read, see reviewed, or hear coworkers and teens talk about. Our skill will grow only if our interest in the service we are providing is strong. Suggesting books and listening to teens' responses is the sole way to know that our pitches are successful. If seven of our suggestions fall flat but the eighth is enthusiastically embraced, we have done our job well because a teen has left the library with a book to read. And even if that eighth suggestion is a flop, but the teen responds with, "Thanks anyway, I think I'll just look around for a while more," we have still succeeded in demonstrating that the library is a welcoming place and that we are willing to try hard to meet teens' reading interests.

Note

1. Neal Wyatt, *The Readers' Advisory Guide to Nonfiction* (Chicago: ALA Editions, 2007), chap. 2.

Part Four

● ● ● ● ● ● ● ● ● ● ● ● ● ●

Special Circumstances

8

●

Readers' Advisory for Homework Assignments

A task unique to readers' advisory for this age group—locating the right book for a homework assignment—may be the only reason a teen approaches the desk. These openings to introduce a student to an enjoyable book are important opportunities to demonstrate both the abilities and the attitude of the readers' advisory librarian.

This chapter will examine

- The importance of treating homework assignments as high-priority readers' advisory tasks
- Interview questions specific to homework reading requests
- Resources especially useful in homework readers' advisory
- Some sample homework requests and how to deal with them

The Problem of Notification— or Lack Thereof

The warning signs are there. First one unfamiliar teen comes to the desk asking if the library has a section for books of stories about the civil rights movement. The same afternoon, another teen about the same age needs help locating Judy Krisher's *Spite Fences*. A day or so later, when checking the shelf for *To Kill a Mockingbird*, you realize all of the copies are gone. Yes, it is the thematic book report assignment again. A flood of teens soon may be racing to the library (hooray!), all in search of the same type of book (uh-oh . . .). One approach is just to show each student how to do a subject search for *race discrimination united states fiction* or *civil rights movements united states history fiction* and let him or her take a stab at the multiple (or scant) hits that result. But this is truly an information need best served by readers' advisory skills. Searching the catalog record will yield any book with the subject heading that applies to the student's need, but it will likely miss uncataloged paperback fiction on the topic. Additionally, many useful and enjoyable books may not have the exact same subject heading and thus would not be included. Consequently, a student's request for materials related to a homework assignment should be treated as a readers' advisory question in order to match the individual not just with a book dealing with the topic required for the assignment but also with a book that he or she will enjoy reading.

In a perfect world, all local libraries would be aware of all local schools' reading assignments. If given adequate notice, most librarians would be happy to pull a modest stack of appropriate books for students to browse. A working relationship with school librarians if you are in a public library, or with public librarians if you are in a school library, is a great resource in this regard. However, even in communities with very proactive school-library partnerships, there are just too many teachers with too many assignments and too little time to notify the library about every assignment that may send students flocking to the library. All librarians, whether or not they have responsibilities in the teen area, should listen closely to requests that could be related to a class assignment and notify their colleagues in that ubiquitous notebook (or other message-relay system) at the desk. The key steps in preparing for teens seeking materials for a homework assignment are summarized in figure 8-1.

In addition to writing a detailed note in the book, leaving a copy of the assignment and any lists that you printed or copied while answering a homework readers' advisory question will give your colleagues and you a head start when the next student comes looking for similar information. Underneath the notebook at our desk, we have a folder in which we store lists that are timely and useful. Having a handy go-to spot for hot topics (e.g., the summer reading list in summertime, mysteries for teens during a genre-based reading

---

Figure 8-1 ● All You _Really_ Need to Know to Anticipate and Prepare for Homework Assignment Readers' Advisory

. . . .

1. Using as many avenues as you are comfortable with, keep your eyes peeled and your ears tuned for possible assignment-related requests.
2. Notify your colleagues if you detect an imminent flood of assignment-related questions.
3. Keep track of the lists used in answering assignment-related requests for future reference.

circle project) saves staff time, helps the whole department stay abreast of the current assignments, and works as a training tool if people look for, use, and add to the lists. To keep the folder usable and relevant, it must occasionally be weeded, with lists filed, tossed, or compiled into polished, annotated documents for in-house publication when appropriate.

The compiled lists can be useful in the long term because many teachers assign the same or similar topics for reading year after year. If someone on staff notices this trend, or finds out from a teacher that the World War II fiction assignment will hit all juniors in early spring, he or she should begin creating a booklist or bookmark for this purpose. Others—especially librarians who work less closely with the material—will appreciate having that information the first time a teen asks a related question. Because books are continuously being published that may fit well in an existing booklist, it is important to revisit the lists from time to time to be sure that the recent Printz winner or a recent book by a hot author is added. If a list is displayed when an assignment is anticipated, or as soon as the library is aware of the need, parents who know that their children need a book on that topic will be able to take the list home. Such lists are ideal for the reluctant teen patron who does not seem interested in interacting with library staff. That teen can simply pick up the list, or a staff member can hand it to him or her. This puts a resource and the decision making very literally in the student's own hands.

If some of your library's staff members have students in the local schools, ask them to let you know if their children receive any class-wide assignments that entail library research. Also notify other departments of a possible influx of teens. Communication between departments is important, especially when working on reading assignments for students in middle school and early high school. Some students, depending on their own or their family's relationship with the library, may not have been in the library since they attended story time as children and may return to the children's services desk because it is the service point that they are most familiar with. Someone at the children's services desk may be able to help a high school freshman looking for a novel longer than two hundred pages set in the South between 1945 and 1969, but especially when assignments are as specific as that, the teen and/or adult services department should be notified that someone may be coming their way soon. Likewise, if a parent brings his high-level-reading seventh grader to the adult services desk in search of fiction set in the Old West, children's services should be notified that other classmates may be looking for similar material in their department. Useful tips for establishing networks to provide high-quality readers' advisory services for school assignments are presented in figure 8-2.

Figure 8-2 ● **All You *Really* Need to Know about Establishing Networks to Identify and Fill Homework Readers' Advisory Requests**
. . . .

1. Deputize your colleagues—any heads-up is helpful.

2. Keep communication open and frequent between the public and school libraries.

3. Do not underestimate the value of your teen patrons, whether they are on the teen advisory board or just drop in to browse. A two-minute chat could reveal quite a bit about their upcoming projects and those of the other ninety-five students in Sophomore English.

Figure 8-3 ● **Three Key Questions for Determining If a Request Is for an Assignment**
. . . .

1. Did someone you know recommend this book?

2. Do you read a lot about the Civil War/Ancient Greece/athletes, or will this be a new kind of book for you?

3. Is this for an assignment you have, or are you reading just for fun?

Is It an Assignment?

When helping young patrons with requests, whether for a particular title or for a less-defined need, it is useful and interesting to ask some gently probing questions to determine if the requested material will be used to fulfill an assignment. As described in the section about readers' advisory interview practices in chapter 5, chatting with patrons while walking to the stacks or waiting for a sluggish computer creates a more friendly experience in general and can yield interesting information, such as how teens find out about the books they want to read. Such knowledge can help the librarian to be more prepared for a potential flood of requests for the same or similar books. Key questions that will help you determine if a request is related to a school assignment are provided in figure 8-3.

Part of librarianship to teens has to be educating teens about the library services—including readers' advisory services—available to them. With each teen interaction, in addition to helping a student find an enjoyable book, we are grooming a future taxpayer and library supporter. Especially at this time, when tech-savvy teens have electronic resources at their fingertips and Google seems to be the answer to everything, reinforcing the unique skills of librarianship is essential both for teens' future as information consumers and our future as information purveyors. A meaningful experience with helpful staff at the library could be what a young voter remembers when visiting a polling place or contemplating an information need in the future.

When teens approach the desk with a reading assignment, they are essentially asking the reference question, "What book meets this information need that my teacher wants me to fill?" It is very possible that the teen does not expect to enjoy the book, so he or she may be unprepared to answer typical readers' advisory questions like, "What aspect of World War II do you think you'd like to read about?" Finding books to meet a reading need is different from pulling up the call number for science fair projects on electronics or books on Ecuador for a country report, but young patrons may not realize the distinction. It is possible that a teen may not even realize that librarians are able to advise on fiction. Unless the librarian clarifies a student's request for Holocaust books by asking, "Fiction or nonfiction?" she could easily misdirect the student from the start.

By taking a request for homework readers' advisory seriously and working hard to find an enjoyable book, you show the patron (1) that you take him or her seriously, (2) that the inquiry is completely appropriate and welcome, and (3) that librarians can answer questions about fiction as well as nonfiction A school reading assignment may well motivate a teen's first approach to the desk regarding a fiction book, so it provides an important opportunity to create a repeat patron by demonstrating how welcoming, knowledgeable, and resourceful your library's RA staff is. Treat this request just like a purely recreational reading request while keeping the requirements of the assignment in mind. In addition to setting the thematic boundaries of the assignment, the teacher may have specified some requirements that you cannot anticipate, so be sure to explore that possibility. Our desk received an assignment for a book-to-film project, but we did not realize that to qualify, the film could not be R-rated. Thinking that we had made the perfect match when we suggested Lois Duncan's *I Know What You Did Last Summer* to the reluctant reader at the desk, we were caught off-guard when she revealed the rating requirement, which obliged us to change direction. Some questions that will help you avoid similar situations can be found in figure 8-4.

Once the readers' advisory process has begun, most students appreciate that their interests are being considered. Others just want any book that meets the criteria and to get out of the library as quickly as possible. Even the student in a hurry will give clues about the type of book that may be a fit. In homework RA, because students will likely come to the desk without preconceived ideas of what they want to read, it is especially important to listen closely to what they say and do not say.

Figure 8-4 • Three Key Questions for Readers' Advisory for Homework Assignments (and Three More for the Nitty-Gritty Details)

1. Did you have a book in mind that you wanted to read [but could not find]?
2. Would you like a book that deals with a particular part of the issue/time period? [The home front or the battlefield? The women's liberation movement or Martin Luther King's involvement in civil rights? A sports book dealing mostly with a sport or mostly with an athlete's life?]
3. Would nonfiction or biographies work too, or only fiction?

Questions for Discovering Further Details

1. When is the assignment due? Do you need to have only the title for tomorrow, or do you need to have finished reading the entire book?
2. How many pages long does the book have to be?
3. Do you have the assignment with you? If so, could I see it?

Obviously, when working with teens who cannot or will not articulate their interests—those whose parents appear to have dragged them to the library, are rolling their eyes at every question, and cannot see beyond the need for *any* book that fits the assignment—you may feel like you are banging your head against a brick wall. However, through their lack of interest, such teens are still telling you something. Ask questions about the last book the teen read, or if he or she reads often, or, if given the choice, what he or she would read. A magazine? The newspaper? Some web page? If possible, build on the answers. Someone who needs a book set around World War II and likes reading *CosmoGIRL!* may enjoy Danielle Steel's *Echoes* for its romance and soap operatic elements, or Bette Greene's teen classic *Summer of My German Soldier.* A patron who seems disinterested in fiction may prefer something strongly tied to an actual event or person, or conversely, a fast-paced, plot-driven novel that is a real page-turner. If all the charm and well-phrased questions in the world produce no results, it is time to turn to the sure-bets notebook, further detailed in chapter 11.

Whenever possible, we try to give the student at least two books to take home and choose from. Sometimes the topic is narrow and it is difficult to find one book, let alone two, and sometimes the student is thrilled with the first selection offered. Generally, however, this is an effective technique that works on at least two levels. At one level, it is good readers' advisory librarianship. There is rarely one and only one fiction book to fill a reading need, and presenting a choice conveys this to the reader. It also displays a willingness on our part to go beyond the bare minimum requirement, just as walking a patron to a book displays a more service-oriented approach than pointing to the stacks. On another level, sending a student home with a choice conveys the message that while we can be a helpful resource and provide good service, the decision of what to read is up to the individual. Librarians may be able to predict how successful a book match is, but only the patron knows for sure what he or she will feel like reading. Especially in homework RA, when a student has sought the help of the librarian in order to meet the requirements of an assignment, we can hope that giving the student ownership over *how* to complete the assignment will translate into a more pleasurable reading experience. Key points to keep in mind when conducting a homework-related readers' advisory interview are summarized in figure 8-5.

Resources for Homework Readers' Advisory

If only we were each endowed, upon snagging that first library job, with an amazing, photographic memory, speed-reading skills, and the years of experience that would enable us to instantly recall every book review, every compiled list, and the whole backlist of titles in our collection. Since this is not the case, readers' advisors working with teens are fortunate to have many useful resources to help with our memory lapses and give us a leg up on the learning curve. These resources come in especially handy when doing homework RA because they are often organized thematically or chronologically.

As a time-saving move, our library staff has worked through several of these reference books, noting lightly in pencil the location of each of the titles we own. This can save quite a bit of time when you are working with a patron. It also avoids the frustration and disappointment that occur when

Figure 8-5   •   All You *Really* Need to Remember about a Readers' Advisory Interview for a Homework Assignment

• •

1. Get to the nitty-gritty of the assignment.
2. Remember that a teen's request for help with homework may be your only opportunity to discuss books with him or her. Make the most of it.
3. Empower the student by providing resources and direction but leaving the final decision of how to fill the assignment to him or her.

you think you have found the perfect title, only to discover that you must tell the student (who, naturally, needed the book yesterday) that he or she will have to wait for it to be ordered from another library.

Although none of us wants a patron hovering over us while we search through a reference book, it is sometimes unavoidable. Combat the feeling of being watched by involving the patron in the search, keeping him or her up-to-date on what you are finding or not finding, asking more questions, or simply chatting about the class the assignment is for, or some other topic altogether. While multitasking may not be a skill we are comfortable with, it is an undeniable reality of working at a public service desk.

NoveList

The subscription database NoveList is dependably up-to-date and accurate. The "Describe a Plot" feature is especially useful when working with teens who have an idea of what they want to read about to fulfill an assignment. Searching for *war Navajo code* was an effective way to find *Code Talker*, by Joseph Bruchac, for a student who wanted to read about the Navajo soldiers who transmitted messages in World War II. Because of the multiple reviews included in most NoveList records, it is a good tool to use if you are unfamiliar with the content of the books. Once you have pulled up a list of relevant records, turn the computer monitor so that the student can view the book jackets and read the book descriptions. This enables you and the student to browse a virtual shelf of relevant titles together. NoveList also offers useful, thematically grouped lists under the "Explore Fiction" heading. Though their suggested age ranges vary greatly, these lists can be useful jumping-off points for exploring subjects, such as Holocaust stories or books about social issues (teen parenthood, runaways, disease), or genres, such as mystery or time-travel fiction.

The What Do I Read Next Database and Books

Within the extensive Gale library are two titles that are particularly useful in homework readers' advisory. Both are available in printed form and by online subscription.

What Historical Novel Do I Read Next?

What Historical Novel Do I Read Next? is a compilation by Daniel S. Burt that's a terrific go-to for requests for historical fiction.[1] Its layout includes a chronological index that refers to concise book summaries, which makes it a great tool when you are working on a booklist. This reference can, however, appear intimidating if you simply hand it to a patron. A more useful approach is to find the relevant section and skim the titles to see if a few pop out as great reads that may have slipped your mind. Because the index does not identify reading levels and authors, it is necessary to flip back and forth between the index and the book descriptions.

The foreword of *What Historical Novel Do I Read Next?* provides another useful feature: lists of best-selling historical novels (organized by author) and historical novels particularly recommended by the author (organized by setting and era). This is a good place to start if a patron is just looking for anything good set in a particular time period. However, the lists include a broad range of books, so a good number may lie beyond the interest or ability of many teens. Be advised also that the recommended fiction list chronologically ends with "The West" for the United States and with a brief and very general section about the twentieth century for the rest of the world, although fiction set well into the twentieth century is included in the annotations.

What Do Young Adults Read Next?

Without a doubt, *What Do Young Adults Read Next?* is organized with teen readers' advisory in mind.[2] You will find indexes of books organized not only by time period, geographic location, and subject but also by grade level and page count. As in *What Historical Novel*, after locating a title in the index, you can use the reference number to find its description. The entry for a title ends with a list of "Other Books You Might Like," which can be extremely helpful if you are working with a teen who hopes to find a book that is similar to one he or she has already read. Of course, even though such recommendations may be great read-alikes, they may not be appropriate for the class assignment as defined by the teacher.

Teen Genreflecting

In the second edition of *Teen Genreflecting*, Diana Tixier Herald has created an accessible volume with the added benefit of *VOYA*-like age codes denoting a book's appropriateness for various age groups, along with brief annotations.[3] The chronologically organized section on historical fiction, the extensive selection of problem novels organized by the problem they address, and the multicultural fiction list will be most helpful for homework readers' advisory. *Teen Genreflecting*, because it covers a broad range of topics, will be discussed in more detail in chapter 10.

Notes

1. Daniel S. Burt, *What Historical Novel Do I Read Next?* (Detroit: Gale Research, 1997).
2. Pam Spencer Holley, *What Do Young Adults Read Next?* (Detroit: Gale Research, 2002).
3. Diana Tixier Herald, *Teen Genreflecting: A Guide to Reading Interests* (Westport, CT: Libraries Unlimited, 2003).

9   Readers' Advisory by Proxy

uggesting books for parents to take home to their children is a common and tricky task in readers' advisory for teens. It is wonderful that parents or other involved adults want to facilitate their children's reading or the availability of books in the home. At the same time, doing our best to suggest books that will appeal specifically to the teens, and not just to their parents, is essential in assuring teens that the library and what it can provide are relevant to them.

Many people may be involved and interested in a teen's reading habits: parents, other family members, mentors through activities or religious groups, and of course teachers. Because the parent-child dynamic is the one that presents itself most frequently to librarians in a public library, whether that adult is a mentor, friend, or other adult, the term "parent" will be used throughout this chapter to describe the adult in the advisory role to our teen patrons.

This chapter will cover

- Tapping the information parents know about their children's reading interests and habits and selecting books that meet those needs
- Suggesting books to a teen while a parent is present—especially if the parent and teen have different opinions about what the teen should be reading
- Coping with the issue of good versus good-for-you books
- Using readers' advisory to maximize opportunities for active parents and busy teens

"Where Are Your Books for Eighth Graders?": Adults in the Library without Their Teens

Teenagers are busy people, so frequently we see parents at the library seeking books for their offspring. Though the parents are doing a great thing by staying involved, good intentions do not always make for easy readers' advisory experiences. How will we know that the books we are handing to the parent will be well received by the teen? In addition, the predictable characteristics of the typical teen-parent relationship can complicate the interaction. Adolescence is a time when young people change and realign their relationship with their parents. They are distinguishing themselves as individuals and sometimes distance themselves from their family unit. It is normal for parents to want to do everything in their power to help teens through these years—emotionally and educationally. They may not always know exactly how or even if their teen's reading interests and needs have changed and may be missing critical information that would be useful to the librarian in suggesting books. Because of this, it is not uncommon for parents to ask for books that are "for eighth graders" or "for freshman girls." It is not that the parents are not aware that their children are more complex and have more varied interests than those broadly defined by gender and age; it is that for the time being, those are the constants that the parents are sure of. Friends may change, musical tastes may evolve, hobbies and athletic interests may be in flux, but from a parent's point of view, age and gender are pretty much sure things. While it may be frustrating for us as librarians to decipher just what the reading need is when all parents can articulate is the bare minimum about their child, it is important to remember how frustrating it could be for the parents not to know the answers to our questions: Contemporary or high fantasy? Humorous or serious romance? Or even more broadly—fiction or nonfiction? When working with parents who are not completely aware of their child's reading interests, rather than being irritated by the lack of clues we have to work with, it is helpful to recall that we and the parents share the same basic goal: to get books into the hands of a young adult that he or she will want to read. Some questions you can use to help parents identify their teens' reading interests are presented in figure 9-1.

If a parent is not looking for a particular book that the teen has requested but is hoping to take home several titles for the teen to choose from, narrow down the field by identifying books that the teen has read recently, or even better, books that the teen has commented on. We can try to use that information as a template for matching similar books, much as we would if the reader herself were working with us. Sometimes, if a parent is not aware

Figure 9-1   ●   Questions That Help Detect a Teen's Reading Interest through a Proxy

1. Do you know what she has been reading lately?
2. Has she mentioned any books she has read for school and how she liked them?
3. Does she read a lot, or not very often?
4. Is she involved in any sports or activities that you think she might like to read about?
5. Has she recently mentioned any topics of interest or social issues that we could find books on?
6. What kinds of movies does she like?
7. Do you recall what books she has enjoyed reading in the past?

---

of what his teen has been reading lately but has a general sense of her other interests, that information can be used as a basis for a recommendation. Just make sure to ascertain that the teen would be interested in *reading* about the hobby or interest. Simply because a teen loves to play soccer does not necessarily mean that she wants to read a book about a soccer player, but it is a good place to start. Consider suggesting a new biography of a famous soccer player, a fiction book that features the game, and another title, totally unrelated to soccer but based on the parent's knowledge of the teen's past reading taste. And if a parent honestly does not remember the last book his teen read, turn to the sure-bets lists, discussed more in chapter 11. Sure bets are the usual suspects of recreational reading: the books that have been favorably received by most people who have read them and can be confidently suggested when we know little about what the reader is looking for. Encouraging a parent to take more than one book home for his teen will often lead to a more beneficial experience—especially when you are suggesting sure bets. These are books that we suggest frequently, so we never know if a teen has already read a title we suggest—or started reading it but did not like it. If you can coax the parent into taking more than one book (some decline for fear of piling up overdue fines), suggest a variety of titles with different attributes: something humorous, something more fantastical, and perhaps a contemporary novel. The key to readers' advisory by proxy is choice. Providing multiple titles also increases the chances of stumbling upon one that will really pique the teen's interest. If we enable teens to make their own reading choices—even if the selection is limited—it empowers the teen much more than if a parent were to come home with one title.

"No, She Doesn't Want That Book": Adults and Their Teens Together

When parents and teens are in the library together, it is usually a great sight for librarians—these are parents who are involved in their teens' reading and help in providing them access to books. Very rewarding interactions can happen when teens and parents actively look for books together, and they improve when parents want their own copies to read. Less encouraging are the cases in which it is obvious the parents have dragged the teens to the library, insisting that they find a "good" book to read. We applaud the attempts of the parents to involve their teens in reading and hope that some of the teens' obstinacy comes not from the prospect of reading but from the horrific embarrassment of being seen in public with the uncoolest of uncool . . . parents! However, sometimes the source could be the teens' awareness that their parents will want them to read something that is not their taste at all. Frequently, the teens in this situation will still leave the library with a book or two, and we can hope that they will enjoy the reading experience. At the least we can use our best customer-service skills to convey to the teens that finding the right book for *them* is our prime objective. An immensely more difficult situation arises when the parent and teen have conflicting ideas of what the teen should—or even *wants*—to read.

In keeping with the spirit of our purpose in readers' advisory for teens, begin by addressing questions and suggestions to the teen, even if it is the adult who appears to be leading the interaction. By speaking directly to the teen, we may find that though the adult has initiated the interaction, the teen is interested and willing to be actively involved once the ice has been broken. Readers' advisory interactions with some shy teens, or those who are uncomfortable speaking with adults, may often begin with the parents taking the lead but can evolve into productive and beneficial conversations. On the other hand, it sometimes becomes apparent rather quickly that it is not the teen who is in charge of the book selection. Perhaps the parent has a specific book in mind that differs from what the teen wants, or perhaps the teen remains unresponsive and uninterested while the parent replies to each question. If this is the dynamic we are faced with, it is the dynamic we must work with. When the parent is the one who approaches the desk and leads the interaction, we should serve the parent's need as it is presented to us. Though it may not be what we believe to be the best way to get books into the hands of teens, our main objective is to answer the question we are asked. If the parent is looking for a certain type of book for the teen, that is the book we should help the parent find. In this situation, it can still help to address questions and suggestions to the teen. Even if the parent is answering the questions, the teen is observing that we are asking questions about reading preference and are attempting to meet the need as it is presented to us, and perhaps if we ask enough times with the right tone of voice, the teen will tell us what she wants. Ultimately, if the book is meant for the teen to read, she will be the one that ends up with it—either in the library or at home. Acknowledging this and attempting to be as helpful and open as possible with the teen is a good way to try to serve the parent and the teen at the same time.

Sometimes we are confronted with two people who are vocal about not seeing eye-to-eye. This is very confusing, and it is all right to say so. Our goal is to serve our patrons, not to get involved in a dispute between parent and child, so attempt to pacify the situation. One approach is to be up-front and say something like, "I'm confused about how I can help you here. Would you like me to find a few different books and the two of you can decide?" The disagreement could really have little to do with books but might rather be a carry-over from an issue at home or one of the power struggles that typify a teen's struggle for autonomy.

When it is clear that the parent is trying to impose specific reading requirements, asking the parent the same types of questions you would ask the teen is the best way to get at the interest or need that you will attempt to meet. Of course, because you are now working with the parent, you could use the readers' advisory techniques and terminology that you use when working with other adult patrons, but we suggest conducting the encounter in a manner that more closely mirrors the approach you take with teens. That way you can hope that one of your questions will prompt the teen to voice a preference. Even if it does not, you are setting a good precedent by demonstrating the way a readers' advisory interaction with a teen would unfold. When you describe a book's appeal factors, it is essential to use the terminology and techniques discussed in chapter 6. Since it is the teen who will be reading the book, it makes sense to describe it in teen-friendly terms.

One of the more difficult situations occurs when the parent rejects a title that appeals to the teen, either due to the work's issues and language or because it is genre fiction or not a "quality" book. Sometimes, objections arise because the parent is seeking a shared reading experience. If *Bleak House* is a favorite from years past, the parent may be sure that Dickens is the right thing for her child, and more than that, she may believe that if her child reads *Bleak House*, they will have something in common, a shared interest to discuss together. Asking questions about the importance of a requested book may reveal such enlightening information. If this is the case, suggesting additional titles that both the parent and the teen could enjoy together is a way to broaden the choices before the pair. If it is more a matter of the parent requiring "quality literature" for her teen, that can and should be respected.

First though, you must determine just what the parent means by "quality literature." For some parents, the classics and only the classics will do. For others, contemporary teen literature that has won awards or been highly acclaimed may be a favorable alternative. Once the type of "classic" is determined, you can treat the request just like any other readers' advisory request. Asking questions about time period, the literary movement, the setting, and other elements that contribute to the appeal of a book will help you find the best match for the patron's request. Some questions that will help you define the kind of book a parent seeks for a teen are presented in figure 9-2.

In an interaction intended to help a teen find a book to read but mainly guided by an adult, it is especially important to emphasize that we love feedback on our suggestions. It is possible that we did not fully understand the patron's request and that the book we provided is not a match. It is also possible that if we emphasize our willingness to find other books if the first book we suggest is not the right one, the teen will remember that and the next time he is in the library, he will seek our help in finding a book that he wants to read. Parents who work hard at guiding their children's reading need to be

Figure 9-2   ●   Questions about Quality

When parents want their child to read high-quality books, they are usually not talking about the binding. Beyond that, quality is a subjective concept and can be difficult to pin down without asking some follow-up questions.

1. Are you looking for a classic work? Something from the nineteenth century perhaps?
2. When you say "quality" do you mean "award winning"?
3. Are you looking for something from a particular era or group of writers?
4. Would a contemporary novel with eloquent language, good character development, and literary motifs like symbolism suit your need?
5. Do you have a book in mind that you would like help finding?
6. We have lists (or books) with titles suggested for college-bound students. Is that the kind of thing that might help?
7. Is there a specific idea that you would like the book to convey?
8. Are traditional or old-fashioned values or moral lessons something you hope to find in the book?
9. Are there elements that the book should not have, like sexual situations, foul language, or violence?

reminded that our goal is to give them what they have asked for—not what *we* think they need—and that if we have not accomplished that goal, the only way that we can improve is if they let us know. At the close of a readers' advisory interview such as this, be sure to make eye contact with both the parent and the teen when mentioning follow-up and feedback.

"Since I'm Already Here . . .": Active Parents and Busy Teens

Many parents have worked a library visit into their weekly routine, but many teens are unable to visit the library due to schoolwork, activities, and lack of transportation. Therefore, it makes sense that parents who have incorporated library visits into their schedules will occasionally look for and take home books for their busy teens. This situation, while it may cause some of the difficulties discussed above, can be used to great advantage if approached correctly. It may take a bit more work to cultivate this type of relationship, but the payoffs will be great—for the teen, for the parent, and for the library. The teen gains access to books that she may enjoy in her scarce free time and all of the benefits that reading offers; the parent gains guidance in selecting books for his child, insight into his child's reading interests, and perhaps even enjoyment from reading some of the titles we suggest; and the library gains loyal support by providing excellent service to its community.

Establish Rapport

The longer we work in our communities, the more families we get to know and the more children we see advance through our services. The toddlers we knew become teens and may come to the library less frequently than they did when their parents brought them in for story time. Frequently though, the parents continue to come to the library on a regular basis without their busy teens. Initially, our reaction may be to lament that we have lost our teen population, that we are no longer relevant, and that these kids cannot possibly be reading if we are not seeing them at the library. While some of this may be partly true, it does not mean that teens are not reading—the research tells us that they do read—and it does not mean that we are unable to assist them. Parents can be willing and eager participants in our attempts to help their teens continue reading books that they want to read but may not have access to due to their busy schedules. Librarians can help by reassessing our traditional role and the mechanisms by which patrons gain information through us and by being more proactive. When we recognize parents who have come to the library without their teens and are looking for books for themselves, we can always ask if they need help finding books for anyone else. It is possible that parents want to take books home to their children but are not sure how to ask for that help. Of course, we do not always know which adults have teens at home. We may be new to the community, the family may be new to the community, or they may just be people that we do not encounter on a regular basis.

When we see lone adults browsing in the teen area, we should approach them just as we would any other patron and offer our services. We should always remind parents who ask for help finding books for their teens that we *want* to help them find these books, that we applaud their efforts at keeping their teens engaged in reading, and that we are there to help. In time, such reassurance and helpfulness could pay off in a beneficial rapport between the librarian and the parent as they work together to find books for the teen.

Follow Up

As discussed previously, the best person to give us feedback that we can use to make better book suggestions in the future is the person who is going to most directly benefit from those suggestions—the teen. If a teen cannot come in to the library, we can reach beyond the walls of the library to bring our services closer to the teen. Rather than simply selecting books for a parent to deliver, we can find ways to connect with the teen. If we compile a take-home list of authors or titles to try next time, we give the parent and teen a tangible product of the interaction. The teen can then reply to our suggestions and send the list back on the parent's next library visit. Bookmarks and booklists, especially annotated ones, if structured correctly, can be great tools for conveying information about specific titles to teens through their parents. Some libraries have had great success adopting and modifying the bookstore model of handwritten "staff recommends" tags for books that are put out on display. Something as simple as a self-stick note with a brief description can work as a mini-pitch for a book that a parent brings home. These short notes relating to appeal elements can boost a book's charm for some teens since it allows them to take the word of someone at the library, not just the word of their parent. The teen patrons of one library have taken to this technique so well that they return the books with their own helpful responses added to the notes.

New and innovative methods of making a good match are popping up all the time. Instant messaging (IM) services such as AOL Instant Messaging and Yahoo! have already replaced e-mail as the primary mode of Internet communication among teens. In fact, a Pew research study discovered that teens view e-mail as a mechanism for communicating with "old people" and institutions.[1] Though libraries are certainly institutions, and we may be considered old by many teens, we do not need to communicate in antiquated ways. We can surprise and please teens by being accessible in the ways that they prefer. Providing IM contact information to the parents of the teens we serve is an easy way of extending the library to teens because they can then contact us whenever we staff the service. Even if we do not offer IM, giving teens an e-mail address at which they can reach us, old and institutional as it may be, allows them to contact us in their time, on their turf.

Broadening the way we think about online communication about books is crucial to staying connected to teens. The Williamsburg Regional Library in Williamsburg, Virginia, has had success with online reader profiles, though they are not specifically designed for teens. By filling out the profiles, teens gain recommendations about books specifically chosen for them by librarians who read and respond personally to their individual interests, preferences, and dislikes.[2] Though we could jot down a few titles for parents who come to the library searching for books for their teens, or print out a list from a website or electronic discussion list based on information the parents provide, teens can receive better results by filling out, at their leisure, forms for an online book-suggestion service (also available in printed form) that, in response, will provide precise and specific personalized suggestions.

The mechanisms by which our teens communicate change as technology advances and as the new technologies become more and more relevant to their personal lives. Libraries should strive to see technological changes as opportunities through which we can be relevant to our teen population. Parents may be more aware than we are of the best way for their teen to send and receive information. We may be able to suggest a system for refining our book suggestions that parents would not think of or are not aware of. Just as important as establishing a trusting partnership with the teens we serve is developing the same kind of partnership with parents who come to the library seeking books for their teens. If we approach parents in a way that demonstrates our goal of providing excellent recreational reading for teens, we can hope that the partnership we forge will not only meet the specific needs of busy teens but also encourage them to come back to the library, demonstrate that we are still a relevant institution that can benefit them in their daily life, and that we are dedicated and trying to help.

Notes

1. Pew Internet and American Life Project, "Teens and Technology: Youth Are Leading the Transition to a Fully Wired and Mobile Nation," July 2005, http://www.pewinternet .org/report_display.asp?r=162.

2. Barry Trott, "Looking for a Good Book? Developing an Online Readers' Advisory Suggestion Service" (program, Eleventh National Public Library Association Conference, Boston, MA, March 23, 2006).

Part Five

● ● ● ● ● ● ● ● ● ● ● ● ● ● ●

Resources

10

Beyond Lists
*Using Resources to Move
Past Award Winners*

●

We have not yet acknowledged the eight-hundred-pound gorilla of readers' advisory for teens. After we conduct a flawless readers' advisory interview but before we articulate the appeal of the carefully selected books, we need to find the books to suggest. Most librarians are aware of the big-name, award-winning books, but they may not be right for the patron in front of us, or one may have been the perfect choice but the teen read it last week. Fortunately, many wonderful resources exist to supplement our personal knowledge. Because we will never have the time to read every title we suggest, these resources do much of the groundwork for us and help us select books based on the interests a teen expresses in a readers' advisory interview. New resources are constantly being released and old standards are constantly being revised, so keep track of what is new in professional publishing and consider adding appropriate titles to your print or database collections when budgets allow.

This chapter will examine

- Print resources for matching books to patrons' interests
- Electronic resources to quickly aid in your search
- Websites with up-to-date and useful information

Print Resources for Matching Books to Patrons' Interests

Teen Genreflecting: A Guide to Reading Interests

We briefly mentioned Diana Tixier Herald's *Teen Genreflecting* in chapter 8 as a useful tool in providing readers' advisory services for school assignments.[1] This supremely useful resource can also help with teen recreational reading. Be sure to note the early chapters, in which Herald relays important information regarding effective service to teen readers and offers tips on building and supplementing teen reading collections. *Teen Genreflecting* is organized by broad genre headings, which are broken down by subgenre, type, or theme. The annotations in this volume make it easy for you to supply information about the books, even if you are not personally familiar with them. Enough information is supplied to convey a sense of the book without giving away important plot elements, and the annotations are written in a style that teens could browse comfortably on their own.

Herald's book is also useful as we create our own reading plans or guide our colleagues through a genre study of teen fiction. Each chapter begins with information about the appeal and history of each genre and serves as a good introduction to why we should want to read the books. Similar information is included for each subdivision, followed by details about specific titles. This volume focuses exclusively on fiction, though its scope is not limited to novels. Graphic novels and books in verse are addressed as a part of the "Alternative Formats" section. Because of its broad scope—addressing eleven genres and many subdivisions within each genre—*Teen Genreflecting* is a good place to start in your search for reading matches. However, if readers want to delve deeper into a particular genre, you may need to move beyond the titles listed to satisfy the teen's book craving.

Best Books for Middle School and Junior High Readers: Grades 6–9; Best Books for High School Readers: Grades 9–12

In *Best Books for Middle School and Junior High Readers* and *Best Books for High School Readers*, John T. Gillespie and Catherine Barr have compiled a massive collection of books, all with annotations and specific grade-level recommendations.[2] Because the two titles have some overlap, with the first covering ages twelve through fifteen and the second covering ages fifteen through eighteen, and due to the great diversity of reading levels within those age and grade ranges, both titles work together to form a complete reference set for serving teens. These volumes are large and comprehensive, and they include plenty of nonfiction titles on everything from sports figures to world population issues to reproductive health. Additionally, almost all of the titles included were reviewed favorably by at least two sources. The volume focused on grades 9 through 12 lists adult titles as well as titles published for teens. It thus accommodates a broad range of reading abilities and is useful for readers' advisory to older teens.

Turn to these books particularly when seeking nonfiction books for teens. The vast number of titles and broad subdivisions for fiction (in the high school volume, the category "Mysteries, Thrillers, and Spy Stories" contains over five hundred titles) can limit the books' usefulness when we do not have much time. The nonfiction titles, which make up the bulk of the work, are divided into sections that are clearly marked and very usable for real-time nonfiction readers' advisory. Within each topic are books that would be suitable for strictly informational needs, whether personal or school related, as well as books with a more narrative style that would lend themselves to recreational reading.

Books for the Teen Age

Created by the New York Public Library for teens to use, *Books for the Teen Age*[3] is published annually and presented in a magazine-like format with covers designed by New York teens. Broad concepts ("The Creative Spirit," "Science," "Here and Now," "One World," and "Action and Adventure") structure its organization, with several lists included under each heading. Excerpts and cover art from some of the books on the list are highlighted. This is an ideal title to include in the teen area, as it easily lends itself to browsing. The newest titles are indicated, and every title has a very brief note about content, as in "3 cool sisters and their interfering aunt" for Dhami's *Bindi Babes*, or "Supple, powerful, long, lean, intense" for the nonfiction book *Tiger*, by Mills.[4] Due to the brevity of its annotations, it is not always the easiest tool to use in the midst of a readers' advisory interaction or when attempting to match a very specific interest, but it can be a great tool to use with teens who just want to browse for a good read. Additionally, it is a helpful publication for librarians who wish to familiarize themselves with popular new titles in a variety of categories. The index of lists, found next to the chapter headings on the first page, facilitates the search for books with a particular appeal or topic. The newest edition of *Books for the Teen Age* can be viewed in its entirety through the NYPL TeenLink website, http://teenlink.nypl.org/bta1.cfm, which also holds slightly lengthier annotations of new titles.

ALA Editions Readers' Advisory Series

Especially for older teens and those who read deeply within their preferred genre, ALA Editions' Readers' Advisory Series of genre reference books can come in handy. Although they are written with an eye to adult patrons, given the high interest many teens have in genre fiction, they will still be useful to readers' advisors working with teen patrons.

The introduction to each volume provides comprehensive but quick and engaging descriptions of books within its genre and subgenres. Thus, using these tools, a librarian can quickly assist teen fans of horror, science fiction, fantasy, and mystery. Because the introductory chapters of *The Mystery Readers' Advisory: The Librarian's Clues to Murder and Mayhem* and *The Horror Readers' Advisory: The Librarian's Guide to Vampires, Killer Tomatoes, and Haunted Houses* speak to the specific appeal of those genres and point out useful questions and ways to discuss the genres with patrons, they are good tools for a librarian to read in preparation for working with teens.[5] *The Science Fiction and Fantasy Readers' Advisory: The Librarian's Guide to Cyborgs, Aliens, and Sorcerers* bundles two genres popular with teens (and often difficult for new readers' advisors) and provides excellent summaries of the many subgenres within each.[6] If you have teens who read romance, *The Romance Readers' Advisory: The Librarian's Guide to Love in the Stacks* will acquaint you with this popular genre and identify many authors that you can suggest to teen romance fans.[7]

The Genreflecting Advisory Series

The books in Libraries Unlimited's Genreflecting Advisory Series, which includes *Teen Genreflecting*, are useful for genre-specific readers' advisory. On the whole, they are comprehensive, up-to-date, easy to read, and well organized. In addition to *Teen Genreflecting*, only one other title, *Rocked by Romance*, focuses specifically on teen interests.[8] It has the same general organization as *Teen Genreflecting* and many of the same appealing features: definitions and information on subgenres, highly readable annotations, and guides to advising readers and understanding the genre. Perhaps additional genre-specific titles will be published in the future. In the meantime, the existing volumes on horror, science-fiction, fantasy, and Christian fiction all either contain sections specifically about young adult material, or have an approach that lends itself to use with teens.[9] These titles in particular are useful for teen readers' advisory services.

The Teen Reader's Advisor

In *The Teen Reader's Advisor*, part of Neal-Schuman's Teens @ the Library series, RoseMary Honnold has created a broad, user-friendly reference for teen fiction titles, sorted by broad genre, with subgenre sections under each heading.[10] Notable are the easy-to-scan annotations that identify the main characters' ages and genders, the story setting, and a suggested range of grade levels for readers. Additional resources for librarians serving teens through readers' advisory are provided in a separate chapter.

Honnold's book also contains a chapter detailing awards given to books of interest to teens, information that can be useful when working with parents who prefer that their children read award-winning books or when trying to meet the requirements of an assignment. Included are descriptions of the awards and where to find additional information about winning or honored books.

500 Great Books for Teens

Substantial and engaging summaries that read like booktalks set *500 Great Books for Teens* apart.[11] Moreover, nonfiction readers will be pleased to find that nonfiction books are given significant attention and interspersed throughout such genre-based chapters as "Humor," "Adventure," "Many Cultures, Many Realities," and "War and Conflict" in addition to appearing in a dedicated chapter, "Information." Useful for librarians, but clear and easy to use, this is a volume that could easily be handed to teens or parents to empower them to choose their own books and to supply a thorough but brief overview of the many flavors of YA literature.

Teen Magazines

The materials discussed thus far are mainly ready references, great for using while working with a teen and trying to find a book. Teen magazines are also excellent sources of information, but they are useful only if we have browsed them before we meet with teens. They may not seem to be expert sources on teen reading, and some of us may be a bit embarrassed to be seen reading *CosmoGIRL!* or *Thrasher* in front of our colleagues, but teen magazines are good sources for learning about hot new books that could be great matches in a readers' advisory interview. Some teen magazines have sections devoted specifically to reviews of books and other media. Publishers of YA lit are becoming quite savvy at marketing books to teens, and it is not entirely uncommon to see print ads for books in teen magazines. Additionally, magazines that highlight teen role models— be they actors or athletes or people in the news—manage to work a question on favorite books into interviews from time to time. Music magazines (*Spin, Rolling Stone, The Source*) are excellent sources for finding out about music-related titles: musicians' biographies or confessionals, retrospectives on musical eras, guides to genres, essays about music, and the occasional fiction title that rocks. These can make great additions to a browsing nonfiction collection. Of course, reading teen magazines definitely can help boost our cool factor. We can also earn big points by being vaguely aware of which

R&B star is embarking on a solo career, who the resident bad girl is on the evening soap, and which angsty teen heart-throb has been seen on the arm of the latest Calvin Klein model. It does not hurt to indulge in a little light teen magazine reading for the sake of staying in touch with the ever-changing world of teens. And besides—they are great fun.

Subscription Databases and Resources

NoveList

Many readers' advisors find the EBSCO sub-scription database NoveList invaluable. It is a fast and effective method for finding books to match a patron's interest, both by subject and, with a little creativity, by appeal factors. Not only does it list almost all of the fiction books our patrons are interested in, but in addition each record has reviews from several sources and a cover image, which helps immensely when working with teens. Searches in NoveList can be conducted by keyword, which searches the entire text of the reviews, or by subject heading. Searching by keyword is quite useful when trying to find read-alike titles. Your patron wants something like Sarah Dessen but has read everything she has written? Searching for *Sarah Dessen* as a keyword will result in several teen fiction titles that were compared to Sarah Dessen's writing in the reviews. Like-wise, because the reviews are searchable, a Boolean search can aid in finding books by appeal factors that are mentioned in reviews. The additional material in NoveList makes it even more useful. Browsing through the "What We're Reading" sections, where professional readers offer up their recent favorite books, can clue us in to new titles we should know about. Book discussion guides for the teen level are excellent resources and are continually being expanded. Award winners and selected subject-specific lists often work as quick-and-dirty aids for staff who are struggling to make a subject match.

Booklist Online

Like NoveList, Booklist Online is a searchable subscription database of reviews. It contains reviews that have appeared in *Booklist:* fiction and nonfiction, for children, teens, and adults. Additionally, all of the feature articles and related lists (read-alikes for a hot new book, spotlights on teen science fiction, romance, or graphic novels) are included and searchable. As of this writing, the database contains current features and reviews back through 1992.

YALSA-BK Electronic Discussion List

Anyone who is seriously interested in brushing up on YA literature and staying abreast of issues related to teenagers and reading will gain much information, and significant professional connections, by subscribing to YALSA's free electronic discussion list, YALSA-BK.[12] The librarians and other members of this list discuss a wide range of book-related topics—from trying to solve stumpers, to collaborating on read-alike or subject-specific lists, to sharing information about book challenges, reading research, and professional-development opportunities. The volume of e-mail can be overwhelming; at this writing, there were nearly eighteen hundred subscribers. However, it is possible to subscribe to the digest format, which results in a lower volume of mail. Also, list members are, on the whole, conscientious about using clear and descriptive subject headings for their posts. This enables readers to quickly scan through and delete messages that may not be of interest or apply to their situation. (Work in an all-girls middle school? Simply delete the many messages suggesting books for senior guys and go straight to the ones on Clique read-alikes![13]) Because of the number and diversity of subscribers, chances are that someone on the list will be able to assist with just about any type of request for help. Another reason to keep tabs on YALSA-BK is that many subscribers are privy to advance reader copies of forthcoming YA fiction titles. For those in libraries with smaller budgets, who need to ensure that each title added to the collection will find a reader, reading a variety of impressions on new books from people in the know can significantly ease purchase decisions.

Useful Websites

Reading Rants

Jennifer Hubert's Reading Rants (http://www .readingrants.org) organizes books thematically, with a definite edge and an awareness of the themes that appeal to teens and the ways teens articulate their interests. She makes no bones about the fact that the site is designed for teens and not for the direct benefit of librarians or teachers. Because of the site's mission, I strongly encourage librarians and teachers to browse and learn from the site. Categories such as "Historical Fiction for Hipsters" and "Slacker Fiction" take an approach to grouping titles that teens are naturally drawn to. The titles of the lists and the descriptions function as ready-made pitches for the titles by describing the attitude and feel of the books as well as their subject matter.

Teen Reads

A part of the Book Report Network of reading- and book-related sites, Teen Reads (http://www.teenreads.com) is an excellent source for book reviews and author interviews of interest to teens and teen librarians. Always up-to-date and full of great features such as highlighted series, new books in hardcover and paperback, and even contests that our teen patrons may want to get involved in, Teen Reads is a good site to bookmark. Reading guides useful for book discussions or inquisitive teens are also included. Individual book reviews are organized by title, making this an informative site to browse both to familiarize ourselves with books for teens in general and to read up on specific titles we have in mind to suggest. Reviews vary in length but are always written in an engaging manner and often include excerpts. One of the great benefits of Teen Reads is its broad understanding of teen literature. It covers everything from the newest works by hot adult authors, to high-interest biographies and nonfiction, to graphic novels, and all are given the same attention as more standard YA fiction titles.

No Flying, No Tights

We have said very little thus far about the importance and usefulness of graphic novels for teens and teen librarianship. Robin Brenner's No Flying, No Tights (http://www.noflyingnotights.com) is one of the best resources for getting up to speed on the newest graphic novel crazes, the classics each library ought to have, and the general age levels associated with various titles. As the site's title indicates, Brenner has created a space where the breadth of graphic novels is discussed—these are not just your grandfather's superhero comics, though the caped crusaders are not completely neglected. Use this site to help teen readers find a graphic novel to suit their reading interest, be it historical fiction, nonfiction, romance, adventure, manga, or something else. Reviewers, although objective, clearly communicate their enthusiasm for the format and excitement about the titles. Especially useful are the age suggestions—teen titles are the focus, with notations for titles especially suitable for younger teens. For older teens and adults, a sister site, The Lair (http://www.noflyingnotights.com/lair/), picks up where No Flying, No Tights leaves off, and for younger patrons, Sidekicks (http://www.noflyingnotights.com/sidekicks/) fills the gap.

NancyKeane.com

School librarian and booktalker extraordinaire Nancy Keane has collected an impressive array of suggested reading lists, grouped by theme (pop culture, African American romance, Christlike characters), readership (eighth-grade boys, high-interest, low-vocabulary, read-alike [If you liked Bridget Jones . . .]), and more in her "ATN Booklists" section (http://atn-reading-lists.wikispaces.com). Lists span youth reading from preschool through upper high school, but the titles of the lists are clear enough that teen books are easily found. Another section of the website, "Booktalks, Quick and Simple," archives hundreds of ready-made booktalks, organized by interest level and subject. Recently, Keane added a podcast feature that allows subscribers to become familiar with a new book each day by downloading and listening to a new booktalk on a computer or portable MP3 player.

YALSA Booklists and Book Awards

Though I began this chapter by encouraging teen readers' advisors to move beyond the books that have won awards, a compilation of useful websites would not be complete without a mention of YALSA's website (http://www.ala.org/yalsa/booklists/). In addition to honoring one book each year with the Michael L. Printz Award for Excellence in Young Adult Literature, YALSA acknowledges many other titles with a broad range of subject matter, reading level, and appeal. The Best Books for Young Adults (BBYA) list includes a great variety of fiction and nonfiction, selected for its "proven or potential appeal to the reading tastes of the young adult."[14] The books are selected with the reading interests of teens in mind, and their appeal extends from young middle schoolers through older high school students.

Another list to pay attention to is the Quick Picks for Reluctant Young Adult Readers, which has some excellent suggestions, both fiction and nonfiction, for teens who are less interested in reading, have not found a book that really grabs their attention, or have difficulty with grade-level reading material. Each year, four thematic lists are released as Popular Paperbacks for Young Adults. In years past, the lists have included themes such as secrets, Westerns, "clean" books, religion, GLBTQ issues, humor, and diaries. As of this writing, YALSA was accepting nominations for the first Great Graphic Novels for Teens list, which should be another useful addition to the already well-rounded group of lists.

Library Websites

You may find that booklists from other libraries' websites are quick and easy to browse while you are in the midst of a readers' advisory interaction with a teen. One of the best parts of librarianship for teens is its wonderfully collaborative nature. Perhaps you have not yet gotten around to creating that "What to Read while You're Waiting for the Next Book by the Author Whose First Book Was Published Yesterday" list. Nevertheless, it is possible that a librarian across the country was so moved by the same book that she has already compiled a list, posted it on her library's website, and there it is for you to use to make your patron happy. Finding lists and other information about teen books on other libraries' websites is easy through simple web searching: adding terms like *library*, *read-alike*, *while you're waiting*, or *recommend* to a search for an author or title will frequently pull up useful lists on library sites.

Conclusion

As time passes, the resources we use to find the best book matches will expand and change. Some titles and sites may become obsolete or disappear, and other excellent ones will appear. Staying in tune with new readers' advisory resources, new mechanisms by which teen book information is conveyed, and new titles that are coming out is of the utmost importance if you intend to provide top-notch teen readers' advisory. Keep current with local favorites by paying attention to suggested reading lists distributed by community schools and bookstores. Browse the book column of your area's newspaper. Stay up-to-date with nominations for your state's teen-selected award list.[15] With each new book or website or magazine article we add to our toolbox for YA literature, we improve our chances of having the right tool to make the right match when working with the teens in our communities.

Notes

1. Diana Tixier Herald, *Teen Genreflecting: A Guide to Reading Interests* (Westport, CT: Libraries Unlimited, 2003).

2. John T. Gillespie and Catherine Barr, *Best Books for Middle School and Junior High Readers: Grades 6–9* (Westport, CT: Libraries Unlimited, 2004). John T. Gillespie and Catherine Barr, *Best Books for High School Readers: Grades 9–12* (Westport, CT: Libraries Unlimited, 2004).

3. Office of Young Adult Services, New York Public Library, *Books for the Teen Age* (New York: New York Public Library, annual).

4. Ibid., 9, 15.

5. John Charles, Joanna Morrison, and Candace Clark, *The Mystery Readers' Advisory: The Librarian's Clues to Murder and Mayhem* (Chicago: ALA Editions, 2002). Becky Siegel Spratford and Tammy Hennigh Clausen, *The Horror Readers' Advisory: The Librarian's Guide to Vampires, Killer Tomatoes, and Haunted Houses* (Chicago: ALA Editions, 2004).

6. Derek M. Buker, *The Science Fiction and Fantasy Readers' Advisory: The Librarian's Guide to Cyborgs, Aliens, and Sorcerers* (Chicago: ALA Editions, 2002).

7. Ann Bouricius, *The Romance Readers' Advisory: The Librarian's Guide to Love in the Stacks* (Chicago: ALA Editions, 2000).

8. A. Carolyn Carpan, *Rocked by Romance: A Guide to Teen Romance Fiction* (Westport, CT: Libraries Unlimited, 2004).

9. Additional titles include Anthony J. Fonseca and June Michele Pulliam, *Hooked on Horror: A Guide to Reading Interests in Horror Fiction*, 2nd ed. (Westport, CT: Libraries Unlimited, 2003); Michael B. Gannon, *Blood, Bedlam, Bullets, and Badguys: A Reader's Guide to Adventure/Suspense Fiction* (Westport, CT: Libraries Unlimited, 2004); John Mort, *Christian Fiction: A Guide to the Genre* (Westport, CT: Libraries Unlimited, 2003); Diana Tixier Herald and Bonnie Kunzel, *Strictly Science Fiction: A Guide to Reading Interests* (Westport, CT: Libraries Unlimited, 2002); and Diana Tixier Herald, *Fluent in Fantasy: A Guide to Reading Interests* (Westport, CT: Libraries Unlimited, 1999).

10. RoseMary Honnold, *The Teen Reader's Advisor* (New York: Neal-Schuman, 2006).

11. Anita Silvey, *500 Great Books for Teens* (Boston: Houghton Mifflin, 2006).

12. For instructions on how to subscribe, see the YALSA website's section on electronic resources, http://www.ala.org/ala/yalsa/electronicresourcesb/websitesmailing.htm.

13. Lisi Harrison, *The Clique: A Novel* (New York: Little, Brown, 2004).

14. YALSA, "Best Books for Young Adults: Policies and Procedures," http://www.ala.org/ala/yalsa/booklistsawards/bestbooksya/policiesprocedures.htm.

15. See appendix C.

11

Creating Resource Lists for Staff

Resource books and online sources help direct our reading suggestions. Librarian-created booklists condense and arrange reading suggestions into bite-size pieces that are specifically tailored to the needs of our communities. Creating lists for staff to use when advising teens on recreational reading material is an essential part of serving teens through readers' advisory. Resource lists enable any staff member, regardless of how much YA literature he or she has read, to assist a teen who is looking for a good book. Resource lists for staff can be thematic, appeal based, or general, but all contain similar attributes that distinguish them from lists for patrons and make them a uniquely useful tool for a librarian helping a teen reader find a book.

This chapter will address

- The four key attributes of useful readers' advisory resource lists
- Sure bets: the teen readers' advisory secret weapon

Readers' Advisory Lists for Staff

Lists prepared by staff for staff can be wonderful resources. At their best, they are focused on genres and types of books that are of high local interest, carefully prepared and organized, readily accessible, and easily used by staff who may not be comfortable or familiar with teen readers' advisory. Every staff member knows about them and can flip to them if stumped for read-alikes for Ann Brashares or unable to think of a survival story writer other than Will Hobbs. At their worst, such lists can be disorganized jottings about titles that the library may or may not own, without such important supporting information as suggested age ranges or appeal elements.

It is not difficult to create helpful lists that staff will greatly appreciate. Well-prepared, interesting lists may interest others in our department in providing service for teens. And most important, the teens in our community will benefit from the greater number of librarians equipped to serve them. The key features of an effective readers' advisory list for staff are summarized in figure 11-1 and discussed below.

Focus

The first step in compiling a booklist is to select its focus. Given all of the possibilities, it may seem overwhelming to limit the list to one particular focus. One way to get ideas is to browse for subjects online at other libraries' websites or at some of the resource sites described in chapter 10. However, looking to our own experiences on the desk is truly the best way to determine the focus of the first booklists we create. Choosing a focus that meets a specific and demonstrated need will provide immediately observable, positive results. Are more teens interested in the Gossip Girl series than we have copies for? Was a coworker recently stumped when a thirteen-year-old asked for horror titles? Has a recent increase in the circulation of Christian fiction titles called our attention to a growing interest in inspirational teen literature? By tailoring our lists to respond to the interests and needs of our teen patrons, we can both serve our community and assist our coworkers in delivering improved service to teens. Even more productive than selecting topics based on our own experience is asking our cowork-

Figure 11-1 ● Effective Lists for Staff

When creating lists of books for staff to use as readers' advisory tools, keep the following features in mind:

1. The *focus* of a readers' advisory list should respond to a local need, often best defined by the types of questions that we or our coworkers need help answering.

2. A list's system of *organization* should suit its focus and be designed with overall usability in mind.

3. To be *accessible*, lists should be assembled and stored in a way that fits the general organizational scheme of the service desk. The lists will be most used if they are easily found.

4. To be *easy to use*, a list should be typed, include call numbers, and provide brief annotations.

ers what kinds of lists they see the most need for. Because they are the lists' intended users, we can hope that involving them from the beginning will increase their sense of ownership in and their use of the lists.

Most lists for staff will be based on a theme or an appeal factor. Thematic lists are structured around a central motif, idea, or topic. They can be very useful when helping students with assignments (as detailed in chapter 8) or teens who are on reading kicks, that is, who want to read every book they can get their hands on that has twins, or is set in Florida, or takes place in the 1940s. Most of the tools discussed in chapter 10 are extraordinarily useful when searching for books that have a certain thematic element or particular setting.

Most resources are based around the facts of the books: the type of character, the time period, the locale, or the main issues discussed. Typically though, we do not read for thematic content; we read because a book appeals to us. And what makes a book appealing if not its thematic elements? A book is appealing because of the qualities it has—its pacing, mood, setting, character types, extent of character development, or amount of detail. Lists, when thoughtfully conceived and carefully compiled, work well to fill the gap between resources based on what books are about and what a specific book is actually like. Sometimes it is great fun to make lists of books whose titles contain the word *party* or are about characters named Buster or have pink and green covers. Such novelty lists may grab the attention of a casual browser but are not useful resources for readers' advisory. We create booklists to have ready references for staff assisting patrons or for patrons who wish to browse for titles on their own. If we keep these two reasons in mind while creating our lists, our results will be more functional.

Organization

The lists that we prepare for staff may be more complex or broad than the lists that we prepare for patrons. Our lists for staff are intended to respond to the information needs of professionals and, as such, may reflect the complexity of those needs. For example, a collection of suggested titles for teens who need to find a book that is over two hundred pages and is suitable for a book report would have a rather broad focus. Nevertheless, it could work as a booklist for staff if it was thoughtfully organized. In this case, a simple, alphabetized list of titles would be of little use as an RA tool. A much more effective approach would be to group the books into categories based on appeal elements, such as books that are fast paced, character driven, edgy, written in alternative formats (like novels written in letter format or as scripts), romantic, or adventurous. In contrast, if the list's focus was limited to fast-paced techno-adventures in the vein of the Alex

Rider series, a clear title and an alphabetized list of titles plus call numbers would be sufficient. The complexity of the organization ought to correlate to the complexity of the topic. A broad and often simple topic may need a more rigorous and complex system of organization than a narrowly focused and specific topic would. The right type and complexity of organization will enhance the focus of the list and ensure that the list can be easily used by coworkers the first time they pick it up.

Accessibility

To be used by our coworkers, our lists need to be easy to get to. If we work with the existing setup of the service desk, we can find a way to include our lists among the ready-reference material that is already there. Does the department currently use three-ring binders to organize information? Would filing the lists alphabetically by topic in a vertical file fit in better with the current structure? Or perhaps archiving the lists online via an intranet or a blog would be most compatible with the way that the department currently accesses information.

The goal is to store the lists in a way that staff is already comfortable with. For instance, we may firmly believe that all of our lists should be archived on a website. This is a wonderfully progressive goal, but it will not be easy to achieve if our coworkers are unaccustomed to searching for readers' advisory information online. We must consider that for our coworkers to gain the greatest benefit from the lists and for our teens to reap the rewards of the department's resources, either we need to make the lists fit into the existing information-gathering schema or we must be willing to assist our coworkers in learning the new structure. Sometimes, duplication may be necessary. Why not provide paper copies in a notebook in addition to starting a library blog for sharing lists? Just as our colleagues have adapted and benefited from the progressing technologies of OPACs and online databases, they can adapt to using lists in more useful and progressive formats as long as the lists provide content that is worth the effort of learning a new system and the system is easy to learn.

Ease of Use

That our lists should be easy to use should go without saying. However, many of us are guilty of jotting down the titles of twelve or so books that would be great for the rush of teens who have been drawn in by the latest TV show craze and may like to read a book of the same ilk. In our haste, we overlook giving our list a descriptive title, checking to see if our library still has circulating copies of the recommended books, or putting the list in a place where our coworkers will be able to find it. Taking the time to clean up the lists that we make, give them clear titles, and put them in an accessible place will greatly increase their usability. Hurriedly scribbling ideas on scrap paper may be a necessary part of your creative process, but it is only the beginning of list making. Lists for staff are professional resources and need to be professionally presented to have the greatest impact.

A good way to start a list-making project is to look to the resources created by other librarians. Frequently, librarian-prepared lists can be found online or picked up at other libraries. These can be huge helps in composing our own lists or may even be suitable for collecting and reprinting as is—but only if we review them to ensure that our library owns the titles and that the structure fits the needs of our staff. Printing out well-organized, focused lists from other libraries and compiling them in an accessible way for our staff is a place to start, but without local call numbers and locations, their usefulness for readers' advisory is limited and they may turn out to be more frustrating than useful.

Another element that makes lists easy to use and elevates them from simple collections of titles to real resources is annotations. If lists are intended to aid librarians who may not be thoroughly familiar with teen literature, the inclusion of brief plot summaries and appeal elements is essential. Annotations save time because they eliminate the need to seek descriptions of titles in the catalog or NoveList. Annotations also can provide a more accurate sense of a book if we draw out the features that play to the focus of the list and could be most appealing to a potential reader. A sample annotated list for staff is provided in figure 11-2.

Sure Bets

We are all relatively familiar with the concept of sure bets, even if we have never heard that term used in the context of books. Described in *The Readers' Advisory Guide to Genre Fiction* as "those titles that appeal consistently to a wide range of readers, from fans of the particular genre to others beyond," sure bets are a readers' advisory lifesaver.[1] These are the books that all different types of readers find appealing and are relatively safe to suggest to a reader who is at a loss to describe his or her reading interests or needs. Sometimes they are described as "romances for people who hate romances" or "historical fiction for non-history buffs," because they rise above typical genre-based appeal and are just good reads. Frequently, these are the books that parents are seeking when they ask for "the books for high school freshmen," as discussed in chapter 9. Sure bets are

Figure 11-2 ● **Sample Annotated List for Staff**

Annotations in lists for staff should be thorough enough to convey a book's appeal and general plot but brief enough that a quick scan will reveal all needed information. Including call numbers that reflect the location of the books is a time-saving convenience. Information about a title should be clear to both staff who know the collection and those unfamiliar with authors or subgenres.

Lurlene McDaniels Read-Alikes

(Tragedies and tear-jerkers, frequently with a romantic element. Often popular with young to mid-teenage girls.)

Bechard, Margaret. *Hanging on to Max*

YA/F/BECHARD

Single teen dad faces the toughest decisions of his life when his girlfriend leaves their new baby to his care. Girl and guy appeal, 8th through 11th grades, sports element, family dynamics, strong and introspective character.

Lewis, Catherine. *Postcards to Father Abraham*

YA/F/LEWIS

Teen girl and star runner faces multiple tragedies: her mother killed by a drunk driver, her brother emotionally damaged after Vietnam, and a cold, distant father. Then she loses part of a leg to cancer. Includes some dark humor, hospital setting, strong character.

Lowry, Lois. *A Summer to Die*

J/F/LOWRY

Young teen doesn't get along with her older sister too well, but must come to terms with her real feelings after finding out that her sister has cancer. Better for younger teen girl, good tear-jerker.

Maynard, Joyce. *The Usual Rules*

F/MAYNARD

After her mom dies in the World Trade Center attack, 13-year-old Wendy goes to live with a father she never really knew and must learn how to grow from and move on after tragedy. Older teen appeal.

McDonald, Joyce. *Swallowing Stones*

PB/YA/F/MAC

Michael shoots a gun straight up in the air, but when the bullet comes down, it kills the father of a local girl. Issues of guilt, mourning, and personal responsibility. Guy and girl appeal, middle school through mid-high school.

Paul, Dominique. *The Possibility of Fireflies*

YA/F/PAUL

When her parents separate, 14-year-old Ellie absorbs the effects of an increasingly abusive, alcoholic mother differently from her older sister. Sad and edgy but hopeful. Late middle school through mid-high school girl appeal.

the books to turn to when we are stumped, and an up-to-date list of them is essential for staff to use in advising teen readers.

At the Downers Grove Library, our sure-bets list has been growing and evolving for years, first appearing as a single handwritten sheet for all YA fiction titles, then slowly morphing into a more organized and broader list, but still stored with the sure bets for our adult readers. This system may work for some libraries, whereas another method, perhaps reflecting the organization of materials already in place, may be more functional for other libraries. A sample of the approach we use for sure bets can be found in appendix B.

Where to Start

A sure-bets list, like the popular authors list discussed in chapter 4, will have commonalities with the sure-bets lists of other libraries but is most useful when tailored to a specific library by those who work most closely with its teen readers. The sure-bets list will be different from many of the resource lists prepared for staff in that it is most effective when each of its books has actually been read. Though it is possible to compile great thematic booklists without reading each of the titles, to be called a sure bet, a book must appeal to a wide range of people, be the type of book that someone wants to pick up and read, and, regardless of its theme or focus, stand on its own merits as a good read. These qualities cannot be reliably assessed by reading annotations and reviews, or even by skimming as described in chapter 4. For this reason, it is recommended that a book be read by at least one staff person before it is added to the sure-bets list. The assessment criteria are described in figure 11-3.

When compiling a sure-bets list, look first at the books that spring to mind as the more popular ones in the collection—the books that are frequently checked out and the ones that teens ask for regularly. These titles are great starting points because they have the legitimacy of the teens' endorsement. It is true that this popularity can hinder their use as sure bets since many teens are likely to have already read them, but that is not reason enough to omit them from the list. If many of the titles on your sure-bets list are frequently checked out, find titles with similar appeal and add them to the list.

Other titles that make great additions to a sure-bets list are those that have held their appeal over time. Teen generations cycle fairly quickly, so the blockbuster titles of six years ago are likely unknown to a great number of the teens currently using our collections. A sure bet will have longevity of appeal. Titles that are very tied to current pop culture trends may be hugely popular this year and function as sure bets in the short term, but they may fade in popularity. The sure-bets list should have a healthy blend of new

Figure 11-3 ● Is It a Sure Bet?

When assessing a title to decide if it should be added to the teen sure-bets list, read it and answer the following questions:

1. Does it grab you from the start? More than other reading, a sure bet should be easy to pick up and become involved in. One of the purposes of a sure-bets list is to help staff make suggestions for teens who are not especially enthusiastic about finding a book to read, are completely unaware of what their reading options are, or have not read recreationally in quite a while. The recommended book should have a thrilling enough opener to keep them turning the pages while they get into the story.

2. Is the book's appeal clear and easily articulated? The sure-bets list is not typically the place for "thinkers"—books that are hard to describe but that people would love if only they gave them a chance. If the appeal of a book cannot be articulated concisely in a readers' advisory interaction, it may not be the right book for the list. Sure bets should be not only good but also relatively easy for staff to describe to patrons in an appealing way.

3. Does the book have appeal for readers of more than one genre? Books that have a little bit of sci-fi, some adventure, and a great friendship or dark humor, a little romance, and some suspense are wonderful additions to the list. With a sure bet, we are not necessarily attempting to find the perfect book for that one person; rather, we are seeking a title that will appeal to a reader on several different levels. A book with a blend of genres or a diverse collection of appeal elements is more likely to attain that goal.

4. Are the library's copies in good condition, or should they be replaced? A recent survey found that what kids really want in their library books are "snot-free multiple copies." Teens are the same way—books should be in decent condition, have an appealing cover, and be more or less readily available.[2] If a cover is badly dated or damaged, or if a title is in high demand and has a mile-long reserve list, consider purchasing a newer copy or some paperbacks.

5. What kinds of books are you excited about passing along? The best sure bets are the books that people can get excited about. They are the titles that make us laugh or cry or smirk or stay up late in white-knuckled suspense, and we want to share that experience with another reader. Ask yourself, "Is this a book that could move a teen the way it moved me?"

titles that show promise and old standbys that are fun, engaging, or moving and that could have been written just as easily in the past year as in the past decade or before.

How to Maintain the Sure-Bets List

Once we have a solid bunch of titles to form the beginning of a teen sure-bets list, it is ready to be used by staff to share information about good books with teen appeal. As has been mentioned previously, the books on a sure-bets list for teens need not be limited to teen fiction. A staff member who has a particular interest in historical fiction, or horror, or science fiction can provide valuable help in maintaining the list. Like the other lists that we prepare as staff resources, a sure-bets list may be better received if we encourage our coworkers to offer ideas about topics and titles. Collaborating to build a well-rounded list that reflects a variety of reading tastes and interests will yield more options for teens seeking recreational reading. As long as staff members understand what makes a sure bet, welcome them to add to the list when they discover a book with strong teen appeal. Copying figure 11-2 and adding it to the beginning of the notebook or folder in which the sure-bets list is compiled will provide a quick check and a useful reminder about the types of books that qualify for inclusion.

Conclusion

Creating resource lists is a win-win project. We become better versed in the titles, genres, and appeal elements of teen literature, our coworkers benefit from our efforts and become more involved in serving teen patrons, and the teens themselves obtain better service. Whether we begin by creating a list for an immediate and specific need or by compiling a sure-bets list, we are doing a good thing for the teens in our community, our coworkers, and ourselves.

Notes

1. Joyce G. Saricks, *The Readers' Advisory Guide to Genre Fiction* (Chicago: ALA Editions, 2001), 8.
2. "Successful New Merchandising and Marketing Trends in Libraries: How They Draw in Patrons and How Publishers and Distributors Can Help Librarians in Their Implementation" (presentation, American Library Association Annual Conference, Chicago, June 26, 2005).

12 Indirect Readers' Advisory and Marketing

The strong influence that our presence in the teen area has on readers' advisory cannot be overlooked. Booklists, book displays, and other pathfinders not only help teens find the books they want to read but also reinforce the concept that finding recreational reading material for our teen patrons is one of the library's priorities.

This chapter will cover

- Developing eye-catching and easy-to-use lists for teen patrons
- Creating big-impact displays—even in tiny places
- Using the Internet to market services and promote titles for teens

Lists for Patrons

Most of the rules for creating staff resource lists, described in chapter 11, also apply to creating lists for teens themselves. Obviously, though, adaptations are required to make the lists teen friendly and to convey the books' appeal clearly. While resource lists for staff are intended for use in helping teens find books, lists for patrons often enable teens to find books on their own. Also, while staff will turn to resource lists because they need them to do their jobs, teens will pick up a list only if it will clearly fill their informational or recreational reading needs. Lists for patrons need to be accessible in a different way than those for staff.

Our booklists for teen patrons need to be easy to use and clear, since it is quite possible that patrons will not approach the desk to ask questions about the books on the list. By creating a list around a clearly defined theme, giving the list an appropriate title or heading, and including useful features such as call numbers or annotations, we can serve our patrons well even if we are not serving them face to face.

A booklist's focus should be clear at first glance. Is it a broad selection of librarian-suggested titles? Do the books have a feature in common, such as a local setting, a diary format, outsider characters, or a music frame? Are the titles suggested for fun summer reading? A resource list for staff may be focused on appeal elements, such as "fast-paced, plot-driven adventures with a good sense of place," but structuring a list for teens in the same way may come off as rather dry, even though the content of the books is anything but. Many of the same themes can be used—and should be used—when creating lists for staff and patrons, but as patron lists are more or less self-service, the focus should spring from the list in a way that is immediately clear. Consider that a teen browsing for a book is likely seeking one of two things: a specific title (or something similar to a favored title) or "anything that looks good." Lists for teens can be focused in a way that meets both needs.

Like resource lists for staff, booklists for patrons can be greatly enhanced by annotations. Whether they are just a few words long or more like a printed booktalk, annotations can save the reader's time by providing some of the information necessary to decide whether to read a book or not. *Books for the Teen Age*, mentioned in chapter 10, provides the briefest of brief notes about each title with great success. Anyone struggling to pare the description of an eight-hundred-page book down to fewer than five words can learn a lot from browsing that publication. Sometimes, its brief notations do not tell the story so much as entice the prospective reader, much as a movie trailer shows us the briefest flashes to give us the feel of the movie. Longer annotations can be useful as well, especially when there is greater variety among the titles in the list. Whereas a list of humorous summer romance novels may not need extensive descriptions for each book, a compilation of historical fiction titles spanning many time periods, due to the variety of its content, could benefit from lengthier descriptions. Sample annotations of various lengths are presented in figure 12-1.

Read-Alikes

Creating lists of read-alikes, books that share appeal elements with books by a popular author and are likely to be enjoyed by that author's fans, are a good way to begin compiling booklists for teens. The "If you like" format works well for teens looking for a specific kind of book and can be useful for those just browsing as well. A list with a title such as "If You Like Tamora Pierce, Try These" tells Tamora Pierce readers exactly what they need to know: these are fantasies with strong female characters and a good sense of adventure. To expand the appeal of the list to browsing teens, a subheading could be added, or the list could be called something

Figure 12-1 ● Brief, Briefer, Briefest

• •

Annotations may vary in length depending on the type of booklist on which they appear. In the examples below, notice that the same material is not necessarily emphasized in each variation of the summary.

Brief

Brief annotations are most helpful when a booklist contains a wide variety of titles or is meant to be studied rather than used as a quick reference. Often, these annotations are useful for describing character-driven books full of nuance that cannot be easily summarized based solely on plot.

Saving Francesca, by Melina Marchetta

When her strong and confident mother suddenly can't (or won't?) get out of bed, Francesca is left to start at a new high school without the encouragement of her biggest cheerleader. Not only is she at a new school, but she's also in the first class at St. Sebastian's that has allowed girls in—and the boys are *not* happy about it. Longing for the companionship of her old friends but forced to forge ahead through less than friendly waters, she finds that she just might be strong enough on her own to stand up for herself and fight for what she believes in, and she might just find friendship and love along the way.

Briefer

Briefer reviews are probably the most versatile: they provide enough information to give a solid impression of the book but are brief enough to be easily and quickly skimmed.

Saving Francesca, by Melina Marchetta

Francesca is one of thirty girls in an otherwise all-guys high school, which she says feels like being either in a fishbowl or invisible. The relationships and issues she encounters are so realistic that any girl could relate to them.

Briefest

The briefest summaries give clues about the content of the book without giving much of the story away. They are useful for lengthy booklists, lists with many books on very similar themes, and lists intended to catch the eye of the casual browser who may not want to spend much time selecting books.

Saving Francesca, by Melina Marchetta

Francesca's new school is an "old boys' club."

---

snappy like "Dragons Are a Girl's Best Friend" or something to play up the adventure element, like "High-Adventure Heroines." Using "If you like," or variations of it, is a good way to introduce readers to lesser-known authors and books by connecting them to the works of better-known authors. Most teens know J. K. Rowling, and many languish between installments of Harry Potter. Using her name recognition to draw the reader's attention to other similar books can work very well. For a readers' advisor, though, compiling such a read-alike list can raise a tricky issue: If a teen loves Harry Potter, what exactly should the similar titles be? Should they be tales of high fantasy with a boarding-school link? Or stories of epic battles between good and evil? Do they need to include quirky side characters and wry British humor? Creating a booklist that is linked to a popular title requires that we make a leap of faith regarding what the reader finds appealing. The best we can do is to choose books for good reason, ensure that they have a strong element connecting them to the central theme, and include an accurate and informative label or title for the list.

Hot Topics and Trends

Another good method for organizing titles into booklists for teens is to think about the topics or themes that are common in books that are popular in your location. Is there a sizable skateboarding contingent that frequents the library (or the steps of the library)? Have you noticed many Goth teens who may be interested in reading about Goth culture or fictional characters that share a similar interest? Is there suddenly a reserve list for a cult classic like *Zen and the Art of Motorcycle Maintenance*? Does your town have a high school battle of the bands or a burgeoning music scene? Any of these thematic elements can lend themselves to booklists. In addition to responding to local interest, useful booklists for teens can also reflect trends or patterns in teen publishing. Novels that incorporate e-mails or instant messaging, books with music playlists, books by authors who have MySpace accounts, or even books that deal with the September 11 terrorist attacks reflect trends that are treated in enough books to merit the creation of a list. By staying in touch with the local teen culture and responding to trends by collecting pertinent books and highlighting them in booklists, you can do a great deal to boost your library's relevance to teens (see fig. 12-2).

Book Displays

Adding a display space—no matter how small— to highlight teen materials can boost the visibility of the collection, increase circulation, and improve the overall look and appeal of the teen area. Displays need not be complex. The most important element is the books—so as

Figure 12-2 ● If You Like . . .

The "If you like" format is useful for calling attention to books with a unifying thematic feature as well as those that appeal to readers of a particular author or title. Here are some handy "If you like" headings:

If you like . . .

animals and their people

big New York style

books that make you think about big issues

Donnie Darko, try these cult classics

emotional roller coaster books

feeling that you're *there*, try these books with great settings

girl-power fantasy

Goth culture and *only* Goth culture

gross-out horror

a happy ending

Harry Potter

mythology

peeking into other people's diaries

quirky British humor (à la *Monty Python*)

reading about teens who really rock

reading the sports page

real science in your sci-fi

scaring yourself silly

solving mysteries

---

long as the books are front and center and accessible, the display is well on its way to being effective. Good displays can showcase books in a minimum of space—just an empty foot or so on a shelf is enough to place two hot new titles face out, or a pair of books on baseball or ballet. Some libraries label their displays, some have dedicated furniture units or holders, and others just let the books speak for themselves. As long as the display is visible and the books are highlights of the collection, the purpose has been served.

Arranging display books in a predetermined pattern, such as moving remaining books to the right of a countertop display and adding new items on the left, enables us to know which titles are duds and are not the right ones for displays. If a book has been on a display for a week or two, even though it is usually very popular, consider removing it and adding something fresh to make better use of the space. If the title that is not picked up is a great read but perhaps looks a little worse for wear, consider seeking out a paperback copy or rebinding it. In addition to providing patrons with easy access to great books, displays provide a quantifiable measure of the success of our teen readers' advisory service. Keeping track of how many books are added to displays, how many displays are created or changed each month, and even how many questions were inspired by display topics can yield useful statistics for the department.

Selecting Books for Display

Books that are selected to go on displays in the teen area should meet two criteria: they should be nice looking—no drab green covers—and they should be worth recommending. In libraries where collection development policies require each title added to have two positive reviews, selecting books should be an easy job. If all of the books in the collection were purchased on the basis of multiple positive reviews, it would be hard to choose a bad one. If the collection is larger or more all encompassing, choosing titles may require a bit more thought. In this situation, select books that you or others have read and enjoyed. As mentioned earlier, asking for suggestions from any teens who happen to be browsing in the area not only helps to strike up a potential readers' advisory conversation but also results in a recommendation that is straight from the horse's mouth. Books that are new additions to the collection make good display choices: the reviews should be fresher in your mind and the covers should be cleaner and brighter than those of older titles.

Thematic Displays

Since many of us tend to display the same great titles again and again, we can add variety by creating a thematic display from time to time. If space permits, running a thematic display and a general one at the same time will provide material both for teens whose interest is piqued by the topic and for those whose interests lie elsewhere. Thematic displays allow us to branch out from the usual suspects and highlight different aspects of the teen collection. Incorporating graphic novels, adult fiction, nonfiction, and even magazines or comic books into thematic displays will draw in teens who may feel that YA lit does not meet their specific reading interests. Moreover, deciding on topics and creating thematic displays can be great fun and provide an opportunity to see just how popular (or unpopular) various themes are in your area. Some sample display topics are presented in figure 12-3, and some possible locations for displays are suggested in figure 12-4.

Internet Marketing

If your library has a website, it is a great tool for marketing readers' advisory services to teens. Dedicating a section of the website to teens, and to readers' advisory for teens in particular, extends the boundaries of the library to the realm in which many teens spend much of their time. Booklists, reading recommendations, reviews of YA titles, and

Figure 12-3 • **Display Topics to Get You Started**

• •

If a display will be out for any length of time, its theme should be broad enough to provide an ample number of titles to last the entire period yet specific enough that patrons will have a sense of what might be included. If you plan to change your display every two weeks for a full year, you will need twenty-six different themes. Here are some suggestions:

All Action, All the Time
Award Winners
Banned in the U.S.A.
Best Books from Last Year
Chick Lit
City Life
Coming of Age
Fantasy—New and Old
Friendship: The Good, the Bad, and the Ugly
Gearing up for College
The Great Outdoors
Hollywood Reads
The Horror . . .
I Never Knew That! (trivia and/or books with interesting frames)

New Fiction
Real-Life Romance
Score! (sports fiction and nonfiction)
Short and Sweet (short stories and brief books)
Teen Advisory Board Favorites
Teens in Crisis
Things That Go Bump in the Night
Three-Hanky Reads
Top Secrets
Way Back When . . . (historical fiction, nonfiction, and/or time travel)
When Pigs Fly: Futuristic Fiction
Winter Reads

---

even a section where teens can submit their own reviews have all been effectively used on library websites for teens. If teens can go online to find reading suggestions, read reviews, browse titles, even peruse virtual displays and place holds on desired books from home, the library website becomes integrated into their lives. Adding a participatory element, such as book-related IM chats with librarians or a mechanism that enables users to contribute their own reviews, will give teens a greater stake in the site and even encourage a sense of ownership in it. Sharing reviews online is fast becoming one of teens' preferred ways of finding out about books. Libraries that recognize such trends can bring themselves into the equation by using their websites to provide expert, book-related help to teens and to communicate their openness to sharing books on the teens' own terms. We would all love to see more teens using our teen areas—and though a website is not a substitute for a well-planned, well-stocked teen area, viewing it as an *extension* of the teen area can both improve the website and increase its traffic and usability. If your library has not yet allocated a section of its website to teens—it should

Figure 12-4 ● Finding Space for Displays
. . . .

Even the smallest teen areas have *some* space to display teen books. Here are some suggestions:

On top of lower shelving units, such as those frequently used for
reference books
At the ends of ranges of shelves
On an empty, eye-level shelf cleared by shifting books somewhere else
On the corner or less-used end of a service desk
On a book cart
On small tables
In slat-wall units at the ends of shelving ranges
Next to catalog computers (or on top of card catalog units)
In dedicated display units

do so now! If the structure of your library's website does not allow the addition of a separate page expressly for teens, consider creating an online presence through one of the free blogging programs, or even through MySpace .com. Booklists, links to author events, and photos of the teen area and teen programs can all be added to a blog with a minimum of technical know-how. Some library websites that do an outstanding job of encouraging teens to read are highlighted in figure 12-5.

Conclusion

We sometimes worry that if we are not actively engaging with a teen patron and discussing books, our readers' advisory service is not effective. Our ideal interaction *is* face-to-face in most cases: this allows an efficient and accurate exchange of information. However, we really can provide worthwhile readers' advisory services for our teen patrons in other ways. By providing useful and interesting booklists, by collecting great books into a browsable display, and by maintaining an active and dynamic web presence, we are still working toward our main objective of connecting teens and good books. Indirect readers' advisory tools and techniques enable us to serve teens who may not be aware that they can talk to us about books to read for fun and to reach teens who choose not to talk with us due to shyness, an interest in a sensitive subject, or any number of other reasons. Developing an eclectic assortment of indirect readers' advisory techniques is essential if we are to be equitable in our service and reach as many teens as possible in the ways that they prefer to be served.

Review and React

http://www.reviewandreact.com
The Buffalo High School, in Buffalo, Minnesota, has structured its website not only to showcase titles of interest to teens but also to allow teens to comment on and react to the books' reviews and to each other's impressions of the books.

Teen Central Online

http://downersgrovelibrary.org/teencentral/
The virtual home of Teen Central at the Downers Grove Public Library offers reviews by librarians and links to websites for book lovers. "Our Picks and Pans" features reviews of books, CDs, movies, and websites written by members of the Teen Advisory Board.

Read On

http://www.hclib.org/teens/read.cfm
The website of the Hennepin County Library System offers many thematic booklists as well as a review form for teens. The "Book Reviews by Teens" section allows users to see all the reviews a particular teen has written as well as multiple reviews for specific titles. To encourage teens to submit reviews over the summer, review writers are automatically entered in a weekly drawing for a free book.

Reads 4 Teens

http://reads4teens.org
The teen website of Carmel Clay Public Library in Indiana provides a structured review form and allows users to comment, similar to the way a blog is structured. New reviews are highlighted, and a Top Ten feature showcases the ten books that received the most hits in the previous month.

Appendix A

● ● ● ● ● ● ● ● ● ● ● ● ● ● ● ●

Popular Authors Lists

The YA popular authors lists were created as a training tool for the Downers Grove Public Library's readers' advisory staff and are a growing and changing work. The list as a whole consists of three broad genre lists. Within each broad genre are subgenre lists of five authors each, with the benchmark author listed first, highlighted by an asterisk, and the others following alphabetically. The authors were chosen based on several criteria. First, each author should still be producing work (with the singular exception of Robert Cormier, who, at this writing, remains the benchmark author of teen psychological suspense). Second, each author should have written at least two books suitable for teens. And third, each author's work should be highly acclaimed, very popular, or representative of its genre. Because the lists were created in mid-2006 with a specific public library's teen clientele in mind, they will need to be revised to match the popular interests of your community. Then, because YA literature is constantly evolving and the field of authors writing quality literature is quickly expanding, the lists will need to be updated frequently.

Realism

Young Women's Lives and Relationships
These novels reflect the many aspects of young women's lives: family, friends, relationships, and coming-of-age.

1. Ann Brashares*
2. Deb Caletti
3. Sarah Dessen
4. Adele Griffin
5. Carolyn Mackler

Working Through Issues
Sometimes called "problem novels," the works of these authors focus on teens who are faced with and attempt to overcome a range of difficult issues.

1. Alex Flinn*
2. Laurie Halse Anderson
3. Sharon Draper
4. E. R. Frank
5. Janet Tashjian

True Stories
Many teens prefer nonfiction. This is a small sampling of authors who have written multiple nonfiction titles popular with teens.

1. Dave Pelzer*
2. Jack Canfield and Mark Victor Hansen
3. Livia Bitton Jackson
4. Jon Krakauer
5. Louis J. Rodriguez

Coming of Age
Not as issue-laden as the books in the "Working Through Issues" category, the works by the following authors incorporate many elements of the teen experience into slice-of-life stories.

1. Chris Crutcher*
2. Joan Bauer
3. Garret Freymann-Weyr
4. A. M. Jenkins
5. Ellen Wittlinger

Teens and Diversity
These authors illuminate the lives, struggles, and relationships of teens whose cultures or identities are often underrepresented in teen literature.

1. Walter Dean Myers*
2. Julie Anne Peters
3. Alex Sanchez
4. Gary Soto
5. Jacqueline Woodson

Historical Fiction

These authors write books set in and accurately representing life in other times.

1. Ann Rinaldi*
2. Avi
3. Joseph Bruchac
4. Michael Cadnum
5. Celia Rees

General Fiction

Teen Chick-Lit

These titles, very often humorous, are mainly concerned with romance but also address social status and friendship. Though the authors listed here write series, not all books in this category are in series.

1. Louise Rennison*
2. Meg Cabot
3. Zoey Dean
4. Lisi Harrison
5. Cecily von Ziegesar

Guy-Friendly Humor

These authors write generally non-romance-based books with humor or humorous elements that have broad appeal for both genders.

1. Gordan Korman*
2. Christopher Paul Curtis
3. Ronald Koertge
4. David Lubar
5. Ned Vizzini

Thrillers

In books by the authors below, teens are in a position of peril or act to prevent others from succumbing to a peril. They often contain a mystery element.

1. Kevin Brooks*
2. Elaine Marie Alphin
3. Joan Lowery Nixon
4. Carol Plum-Ucci
5. Nancy Werlin

Psychological Suspense

These authors' books also contain an element of peril, but it is often perpetrated psychologically or exists mainly in the character's mind.

1. Robert Cormier*
2. Gail Giles
3. Pete Hautman
4. Kathe Koja
5. Terry Trueman

Literary

These authors employ more literary elements than most authors for teens do. Their writing is evocative and the content lends itself well to discussion.

1. Angela Johnson*
2. Joyce Carol Oates
3. Adam Rapp
4. Sonya Sones
5. Markus Zusak

Action/Adventure

In these authors' fast-paced novels, teens are active agents in saving or rescuing themselves and others, which frequently plays out as one against the elements.

1. Anthony Horowitz*
2. Orson Scott Card
3. Nancy Farmer
4. Will Hobbs
5. Ben Mikaelsen

Speculative Fiction

Urban Fantasy

Books by the following authors are often dark and urban, with fantasy elements integrated into modern life.

1. Garth Nix*
2. Eoin Colfer
3. Charles de Lint
4. Neil Gaiman
5. Philip Pullman

High Fantasy

These authors incorporate classical fantasy elements, structure, and motifs into their often heroic tales.

1. J. K. Rowling*
2. Robert Jordan
3. Mercedes Lackey
4. Christopher Paolini
5. Tamora Pierce

Fairy Tales, New and Old

These authors specialize in reinventing or retelling classic fairy tales or creating new ones. Many of their books contain elements of magic realism.

1. Donna Jo Napoli*
2. Alice Hoffman
3. Robin McKinley
4. Vivian Vande Velde
5. Jane Yolen

Horror

Whether through supernatural means or not, books by these authors aim to scare or gross out teen readers.

1. Darren Shan*
2. Jan Harold Brunvand
3. Stephen King
4. Dean Koontz
5. Neal Shusterman

Vampires and Otherworldly Creatures

The following authors write about characters who struggle with their identities as otherworldly creatures or with their relationships to such beings.

1. Amelia Atwater-Rhodes*
2. Holly Black
3. Libba Bray
4. Annette Curtis Klause
5. Stephenie Meyer

Science Fiction

Stories by these authors take place in an imaginary world founded on scientific possibilities or in our realistic world with scientific concepts accelerated and are often driven by issues that those scientific possibilities create.

1. Anne McCaffrey*
2. Ann Halam
3. Philip Reeve
4. Star Wars series
5. Scott Westerfeld

Appendix B

● ● ● ● ● ● ● ● ● ● ● ● ● ●

Sure Bets

Sure bets are the books that all different types of readers find appealing and are relatively safe to suggest to teens who have difficulty describing their reading interests or needs. They are also probably the books that parents have in mind when they are looking for reading matter for their teens. Sure bets are the books to turn to when you are stumped, and maintaining up-to-date lists of them is essential. The lists in this appendix illustrate the approach we take to sure bets at the Downers Grove Library.

Younger Teen—Character Driven

Alphin, Elaine Marie. *Counterfeit Son*
> Son of serial killer poses as victim; suspense, psychological

Atkins, Catherine. *When Jeff Comes Home*
> Teen returns home after abduction

Atwater-Rhodes, Amelia
> Vampires and shape-shifters; popular with girls, romantic element

Bauer, Joan
> Good-hearted characters, usually with a quirk, who are often on personal journeys or missions

Brashares, Ann. Sisterhood of the Traveling Pants series
> Group of girlfriends who are each very different share a pair of jeans and stories of their adventures during their summer apart

Dessen, Sarah. *This Lullaby*
> Romance and issues

Griffin, Adele. *Where I Want to Be*
> *Lovely Bones* read-alike; two sisters come to grips with changes after one of them dies

Hautman, Pete. *Godless*
> Guy questions his father's Catholicism and invents his own religion, which leads to danger for some of those who join

Hesse, Karen. *Witness*
Racism in rural town in 1930s; novel in verse

Hinton, S. E. *The Outsiders*
Classic story of class rivalry and coming of age

Mackler, Carolyn. *The Earth, My Butt, and Other Big Round Things*
Strong girl overcomes family and image issues

———. *Love and Other Four-Letter Words*
Funny but not too light

McCormick, Patricia. *Cut*
Girls, cutting

Peck, Richard. *Fair Weather; A Long Way from Chicago; A Year Down Yonder*
Gentle and funny; *Long Way* and *Year Down* deal with a brother and sister respectively during the Great Depression

Peters, Julie Ann. *Define Normal*
Middle school; priss and punk girls find common ground

Spinelli, Jerry. *Stargirl*
Guy observes and befriends the most interesting girl he's ever met

Whitney, Kim Ablon. *See You Down the Road*
Gypsy family, teen girl thinking of breaking away

Young, Karen. *The Beetle and Me*
Strong family, a girl and her car

Zephaniah, Benjamin. *Face*
Boy scarred after an accident

Younger Teen—Plot Driven

Avon Romance series, various authors

Bo, Ben. *The Edge; Skullcrack*
Boys; sports

Cabot, Meg. *All American Girl; Princess Diaries*

Carlson, Melody. *Diary of a Teenage Girl*
First in series; Christian oriented

Clark, Mary Higgins. *A Stranger Is Watching*

Hopkins, Cathy. Mates, Dates series

Maxwell, Katie. *The Year My Life Went Down the Loo*
American girl in England; funny

Mikaelsen, Ben. *Tree Girl*
  Adventure and politics in South American country

Rennison, Louise. *Angus Thongs and Full Frontal Snogging*

Sheldon, Dyan. *Confessions of a Teenage Drama Queen; Planet Janet*

Shute, Nevil. *The Pied Piper*
  World War II

Sweeney, Joyce. *Players*
  Boys; basketball

Yancey, Rick. *Extraordinary Adventures of Alfred Kropp*
  Perfect follow-up to *Stormbreaker*; modern adventure play on King Arthur legend

Younger Teen—Fantasy/Sci-Fi

Card, Orson Scott. *Ender's Game*

Farmer, Nancy. *Sea of Trolls*
  Good historical fantasy; Viking era

McCaffrey, Anne. *Dragondrums*

Nix, Garth. *Sabriel*
  Daughter of a necromancer

Westerfeld, Scott. *Midnighters: Secret Hour*
  Teens with powers that come out after midnight

———. *Peeps*
  Vampirism is really an STD

Zindel, Paul. *Night of the Bat* and others
  Horror for young teens; bloody, fantasy violence

Older Teen—Character Driven

Anderson, Laurie Halse. *Catalyst*
  Smart girl loses it after not getting into MIT

———. *Prom*
  "Normal" girl steps in to save prom for her best friend; sex

———. *Speak*
  Aftermath of rape, teen turns to art

Cohn, Rachel. *Gingerbread; Pop Princess*

Crutcher, Chris. *Staying Fat for Sarah Byrnes; Whale Talk*
Guy characters; athletes but not really sports books

Dallas, Sandra. *Diary of Matty Spencer*

Desai Hidier, Tanuja. *Born Confused*
Girl; Indian; American culture; funny

Dessen, Sarah
Thoughtful; girls and relationships

Devoto, Pat Cunningham. *My Last Days as Roy Rogers*
Young girl's southern summer; social issues seen through the eyes of a
child; similar to *To Kill a Mockingbird*

Donnelly, Jennifer. *A Northern Light*
Historical; girl's tension between caring for family and pursuing college

Going, K. L. *Fat Kid Rules the World*
Music scene saves depressed "fat kid" after a "druggie" teen recruits him as
a drummer

Hildreth, Denise. *Savannah from Savannah*
Christian chick lit; college

Hoffman, Alice. *The Probable Future*
Stella wakes up on her thirteenth birthday and is able to see how those
around her will die

Johnson, Angela. *First Part Last*
Teen dad; beautiful language

Letts, Billie. *Where the Heart Is*
Pregnant teen is abandoned at Wal-Mart and finds friendship and support
in the small town

MacKall, Dandi Daley. *Love Rules*
Christian chick lit; college

Mackler, Carolyn. *The Earth, My Butt, and Other Big Round Things*
Strong girl overcomes family and image issues

———. *Love and Other Four-Letter Words*
Funny but not too light

Moriarty, Laura. *The Center of Everything*
Young woman's beliefs about politics, religion, etc., are challenged as she
comes of age

Peck, Richard. *The River between Us*
  Civil War

Roberts, Nora. *Dance upon the Air, Heaven and Earth*, and *Face the Fire*
  Three Sisters trilogy; romance and a paranormal twist

Sinclair, April. *Coffee Will Make You Black*
  Coming-of-age and racism in 1960s Chicago

Vonnegut, Kurt. *Slaughterhouse Five*
  World War II; boys

————. *Welcome to the Monkey House*
  Boys; short stories

Watson, Lawrence. *Montana 1948*
  Young man faces issues of family loyalty in the face of a crime he becomes aware of

Zusak, Markus. *I Am the Messenger*
  Older teen cabbie is sent on missions in his hometown; great for teen guys

Older Teen—Plot Driven (or Fast Paced)

Brown, Dan. *The Da Vinci Code*

Cabot, Meg. *Boy Next Door; Boy Meets Girl*
  Funny; easy reads

Christie, Agatha. Especially *Man in the Brown Suit; And Then There Were None*

Clark, Mary Higgins. *A Stranger Is Watching* and others

Evanovich, Janet. Stephanie Plum series

Gilman, Dorothy. Mrs. Polifax series

Grisham, John

Kinsella, Sophie. Shopaholic series

McNamee, Graham. *Acceleration*
  Teen finds psycho's journal on a subway; mystery

Shute, Nevil. *The Pied Piper*
  World War II

von Ziegesar, Cecily. Gossip Girl series

Zusak, Markus. *I Am the Messenger*
  Teen cabbie is sent on missions in his hometown; great for teen guys

Older Teen—Fantasy/Sci-Fi

Adams, Douglas. *Hitchhiker's Guide to the Galaxy*

Eddings, David

Fforde, Jasper. *The Eyre Affair;* Thursday Next series

Gaiman, Neil. *Neverwhere*

Pratchett, Terry. Discworld series

Appendix C

• • • • • • • • • • • • • • •

Teen-Selected Book Awards

The following is a list of book awards voted on by teens and focused on titles for grades 7 through 12.

Pacific Northwest Young Reader's Choice Award, Intermediate and Senior divisions

(Alaska, Idaho, Montana, Oregon, and Washington in the United States and Alberta and British Columbia in Canada)

http://www.pnla.org/yrca/

Arizona

Grand Canyon Reader Award, Teen category

http://www.grandcanyonreaderaward.org

California

California Young Reader Medal, Middle School/Junior High and Young Adult categories

http://californiayoungreadermedal.org

Colorado

Colorado Blue Spruce Young Adult Book Award

http://cal-webs.org/bluespruce/

Connecticut

Nutmeg Book Award, chosen by Connecticut's children, Intermediate and Teen categories

http://www.nutmegaward.org

Florida

Sunshine State Young Reader's Award, Grades 6–8

http://www.myssyra.org

Georgia

Georgia Children's Book Award, Middle Grade Novels
http://www.coe.uga.edu/gcba/
Georgia Peach Book Award for Teen Readers, High School
http://www.glma-inc.org/peachaward.htm

Illinois

Abraham Lincoln Illinois High School Book Award, High School
http://islma.org/lincoln.htm
Rebecca Caudill Young Readers' Book Award, Middle Grade Novels
http://www.rcyrba.org

Indiana

Eliot Rosewater Indiana High School Book Award (Rosie Award),
High School
http://www.ilfonline.org/AIME/Rosie/EliotRosewaterProgram.htm

Iowa

Iowa Teen Award, Grades 6–9
http://www.iasl-ia.org/teen.php
Iowa High School Book Award, Grades 9–12
http://www.iasl-ia.org/ihsba.php

Kentucky

Kentucky Bluegrass Award, Grades 6–8 and Grades 9–12 divisions
http://kba.nku.edu

Louisiana

Young Readers' Choice Award, Grades 6–8
http://www.state.lib.la.us/la_dyn_templ.cfm?doc_id=83

Maryland

Black-Eyed Susan Book Award, Grades 6–9 and High School categories
http://mdedmedia.org/besall.html

Michigan

Great Lakes Great Books Award, Grades 6–8 and 9–12 categories
http://www.michiganreading.org/greatbooks/index.html
Thumbs Up! Award, Ages 12–18 years
http://www.mla.lib.mi.us/tsdthumbsup/

Minnesota

Maude Hart Lovelace Book Award, Division II, Grades 6–8
http://www.isd77.k12.mn.us/lovelace/lovelace.html

Missouri

Mark Twain Award, Grades 4–8
http://www.maslonline.org/awards/books/MarkTwain/
Gateway Readers Award, Grades 9–12
http://www.maslonline.org/awards/books/Gateway/

Nebraska

Golden Sower Award, Young Adult category
http://www.nebraskalibraries.org/sower.htm

Nevada

Nevada Young Readers Award, Intermediate and Young Adult categories
http://www.nevadalibraries.org/Divisions/NYRA/

New Hampshire

The Flume: NH Teen Reader's Choice Award, Grades 9–12
http://www.nashualibrary.org/YALS/Flume.htm
Isinglass Teen Read Award, Grades 7–8
http://metrocast.net/~blibrary/teenindex.htm

New Jersey

Garden State Book Awards, Fiction, Grades 6–8; Fiction, Grades 9–12;
and Nonfiction categories
http://www.njla.org/honorsawards/book/teen.html

New Mexico

Land of Enchantment, Young Adult category
http://www.loebookaward.com

New York

Charlotte Award, Young Adult category
http://www.nysreading.org/Awards/charlotte/index.html

Ohio

Teen Buckeye Book Award, Grades 9–12
http://www.bcbookaward.info/teens/
Buckeye Children's Book Award, Grades 6–8
http://www.bcbookaward.info

Oklahoma

Sequoyah Book Awards, Young Adult category
http://www.oklibs.org/sequoyah/

Pennsylvania

Pennsylvania Young Reader's Choice Award, Grades 6–8 and
Young Adult categories
http://www.psla.org/grantsandawards/pyrca.php3

Rhode Island

Rhode Island Teen Book Award, Ages 12–18 years
http://www.yourlibrary.ws/ya_webpage/ritba/ritbaindex.htm

South Carolina

SCASL Young Adult Book Awards, Grades 9–12
http://www.scasl.net/bkawards/yaba.htm
SCASL Junior Book Awards, Grades 6–9
http://www.scasl.net/bkawards/jba.htm

Tennessee

Volunteer State Book Award, Grades 7–12
http://www.discoveret.org/tasl/vsba.htm

Utah

Beehive Awards, Young Adult category
http://www.clau.org

Virginia

Virginia Readers' Choice, Middle School (Grades 6–9) and High School (Grades 10–12) levels
http://www.vsra.org/VRCindex.html

Washington

Evergreen Young Adult Book Award, Grades 7–12
http://www.kcls.org/evergreen/

Wisconsin

Golden Archer Award, Middle/Junior High School category
http://www.wemaonline.org/ag.ga.overview.cfm

Wyoming

Soaring Eagle Book Award, Grades 7–12
http://www.ccpls.org/html/soaringeagle.html

Glossary

Accelerated Reader   A program used mainly in schools to track and monitor the reading habits of students. Books are assigned readability levels, students take quizzes after reading the books, and data gathered from the quizzes are collected.

ALA   The American Library Association. The main professional organization for librarians in the United States, encompassing many divisions with emphases on various elements of librarianship.

anime   Animated films of a style that originated in Japan. Some anime titles have a manga counterpart.

appeal   In readers' advisory terms, the elements of a book that prove satisfying to a reader. Examples of appeal are fast pace, interesting characters, dark humor, futuristic setting.

benchmark author   An author whose work in a genre is the standard to which other works in that genre are compared.

booktalk   An impromptu or planned description of a book designed to entice a potential reader. Sometimes, many books are presented at once in a formal setting, and other times, a booktalk is limited to one title that a patron has inquired about. Some booktalks are elaborate and staged, with props or dramatics, and others are simple, brief, and unassuming.

character   The type of people in a book, but also the depth with which the players in a story are depicted. Also used in place of characterization.

classics   Books generally considered by a group of people to be important titles that will stand the test of time. The nature and quality of books identified as classics will vary depending on who describes them as such and for what purpose. For example, classics of sci-fi defined by die-hard aficionados will differ from classics of romantic poetry defined by English professors. Describing a book as a classic for the purposes of readers' advisory can be problematic in the same way that describing a book as well written is, because the definition and understanding of the term changes from person to person.

coming-of-age   The point or process of transition from childhood to adulthood. Much teen literature has an element of coming-of-age because teens are very often struggling to understand themselves and the world in new ways as their maturity increases.

frame   The setting of a book, but also other elements that add to the experience of reading: the type and level of detail, the tone of the narrative, and the literary devices used to tell the story (as in epistolary novels or novels written in verse).

generalist   A librarian who fulfills many roles in the library, doing readers' advisory work as well as reference, circulation, programming, and/or technical processing. Also librarians who work with a wide variety of ages.

IM   Instant messaging, a manner of communicating through text conversations conducted online that is very popular with teenagers. A variety of services, such as America Online (AIM), Yahoo! Messenger, and ICQ, offer free IM.

manga   A style of drawing comics popularized in Japan. Also refers to the graphic novels drawn in this style. *See also* anime.

MySpace.com   One of many social networking sites popular with young people. Individuals create personal web pages, network, and sometimes meet in person through sites such as this. The anonymity of such social networking sites has led to concerns about Internet safety for teens who use them.

OPAC   An online public access catalog. Often referred to as an online catalog or by the name of the product or group providing the catalog service.

pacing   The relative speed with which a story moves along. Fast-paced books are often plot based and move quickly, pulling the reader through the narrative, while slower paced books often contain more detail over which the reader will linger.

page-turner   A book that through its fast pace and compelling story literally keeps readers turning the pages.

patron   A person who uses the library. Sometimes called customers or clients.

pitch   In readers' advisory terms, what we do when we convey information about a book to a patron in a way that attempts to entice him or her to read it. Similar to a booktalk, but a pitch typically consists of quickly describing several books to a patron, which are presented as options for further examination or for checking out.

plot   The sequence of events in a book that combine to create a story.

proxy   A person who stands in the stead of another. In readers' advisory, used to describe a person who is attempting to find recreational reading material for a teen who is not present.

RA   Readers' advisory.

Ranganathan's laws   Five laws proposed by S. R. Ranganathan (1892–1972) that are intended to summarize the purpose and intent of libraries. Since their popularity has spread and the breadth of librarianship has expanded, they have been added to and adapted in a variety of ways. The original five laws were (1) Books are for use; (2) Every reader his or her book; (3) Every book its reader; (4) Save the time of the reader; (5) The library is a growing organism.

readers' advisory   The process and skill of aiding patrons in finding suitable recreational reading by detecting their reading interest, finding books to match that interest, and articulating the books' appeal.

reading level   The assessed relative ease or difficulty of reading a particular book. Many different methods have been devised to assess the reading level of books, but librarians and teachers frequently use the average grade level in school to describe a book's readability.

recreational reading   Reading done for enjoyment and pleasure. Not reading that has been assigned or is required. Sometimes described as self-selected reading.

self-selected reading   Reading material chosen by the reader, whether based on requirements from others, chosen from a previously selected list, or found completely autonomously. Self-selected reading is often, but not always, recreational reading.

TAB.   Teen advisory board. A group of local teenagers who advise the library on how to increase its appeal to teens, do special projects with the library, and/or are involved in the young adult collection or space.

TAG   Teen advisory group. *See* TAB.

teens   Adolescents between twelve and eighteen years of age, though sometimes for the purpose of library service, teen services extend to patrons in their early twenties. The term for this age group preferred by many of its members.

YA   Young adults. A term very frequently used in library circles to refer to the age group that includes twelve- through eighteen- (or twenty-two-) year-olds. Also frequently used to describe the books written for and marketed to this age group.

YALSA   The Young Adult Library Services Association. A division of ALA focused on serving teens.

Bibliography

Abrams, Liesa. "Talkin' Teen." *Writers Digest* 85, no. 11 (2005): 56–57.

Adult Reading Round Table Steering Committee. "ARRT Young Adult Genre Fiction List." Adult Reading Round Table of Illinois, 2002.

Bernier, Anthony, Mary K. Chelton, Christine A. Jenkins, and Jennifer Burek Pierce, comps. "Two Hundred Years of Young Adult Library Services History." e-VOYA web-only article, full-length web version (June 2005). http://www.voya.com/whatsinvoya/web_only_articles/Chronology_200506.shtml.

Brown, Dave F. "The Significance of Congruent Communication in Effective Classroom Management." *Clearing House* 79 (September/October 2005): 13–14.

Burt, Daniel S. *What Historical Novel Do I Read Next?* Detroit: Gale Research, 1997.

Carpan, A. Carolyn. *Rocked by Romance: A Guide to Teen Romance Fiction.* Westport, CT: Libraries Unlimited, 2004.

Cart, Michael. *From Romance to Realism: 50 Years of Growth and Change in Young Adult Literature.* New York: HarperCollins, 1996.

Chelton, Mary K. *Bare Bones: Young Adult Services, Tips for Public Library Generalists.* Chicago: ALA Editions, 1993.

Cunningham, A. E., and K. E. Stanovich. "What Reading Does for the Mind." *American Educator* 22, no. 1 (Spring/Summer 1998): 8–15.

Edwards, Margaret A. *The Fair Garden and the Swarm of Beasts: The Library and the Young Adult.* Reprint. Chicago: ALA Editions, 1994.

Evans, G. Edward, Anthony J. Amodeo, and Thomas L. Carter. *Introduction to Library Public Services.* 6th ed. Greenwood, CO: Libraries Unlimited, 1999.

Gillespie, John T., and Catherine Barr. *Best Books for High School Readers: Grades 9–12.* Westport, CT: Libraries Unlimited, 2004.

———. *Best Books for Middle and Junior High School Readers: Grades 6–9.* Westport, CT: Libraries Unlimited, 2004.

Green, Samuel Swett. "Personal Relations between Librarian and Readers." *American Library Journal* 1 (1876): 74.

Herald, Diana Tixier. *Teen Genreflecting: A Guide to Reading Interests.* Westport, CT: Libraries Unlimited, 2003.

Holley, Pam Spencer. "President's Message: Fall [2005] YALS." Young Adult Library Services Association. http://www.ala.org/ala/yalsa/fall .htm.

———. *What Do Young Adults Read Next?* Detroit: Gale Research, 2002.

Honnold, RoseMary. *The Teen Reader's Advisor.* New York: Neal-Schuman, 2006.

Hutchinson, Margaret. "Fifty Years of Young Adult Reading, 1921–1971." In *Young Adult Literature in the Seventies: A Selection of Readings,* edited by Jana Varlejs, 39–69. Metuchen, NJ: Scarecrow Press, 1978.

Jones, Patrick. *Connecting Young Adults and Libraries.* New York: Neal-Schuman, 2004.

———. *A Core Collection for Young Adults.* New York: Neal-Schuman, 2003.

Krashen, Stephen D. "The Power of Reading: Insights from the Research." 2nd ed. Westport, CT: Libraries Unlimited, 2006.

Mackey, Margaret. "Risk, Safety, and Control in Young People's Reading Experiences." *School Libraries Worldwide* 9, no. 1 (2003): 50–63.

Management of Reference Committee. "Guidelines for Behavioral Performance of Reference and Information Service Providers." *RUSA Reference Guidelines.* RUSA Board of Directors, 2004. http://www.ala. org/ala/rusa/rusaprotools/referenceguide/guidelinesbehavioral.htm.

Martin, June, Michael Romas, Marsha Medford, Nancy Leffert, and Sherry L. Hatcher. "Adult Helping Qualities Preferred by Adolescents." *Adolescence* 41 (Spring 2006): 127–38.

McGrath, Renée Vaillancourt, ed. *Excellence in Library Services to Young Adults.* 4th ed. Chicago: ALA Editions, 2004.

New York Public Library Office of Young Adult Services. *Books for the Teen Age.* New York: annual.

Nippold, Marilyn A., Jill K. Duthie, and Jennifer Larsen. "Literacy as a Leisure Activity: Free-Time Preferences of Older Children and Young Adults." *Language, Speech, and Hearing Services in Schools* 36 (2005): 93–102.

Pew Internet and American Life Project. "Teens and Technology: Youth Are Leading the Transition to a Fully Wired and Mobile Nation" (July 2005). http://www.pewinternet.org/report_display.asp?r=162.

Ross, Catherine Sheldrick, Lynne McKechnie, and Paulette M. Rothbauer. *Reading Matters: What the Research Reveals about Reading, Libraries, and Community*. Westport, CT: Libraries Unlimited, 2006.

Saricks, Joyce G. *The Readers' Advisory Guide to Genre Fiction*. Chicago: ALA Editions, 2001.

———. *Readers' Advisory Service in the Public Library*. 3rd ed. Chicago: ALA Editions, 2005.

Silvey, Anita. *500 Great Books for Teens*. Boston: Houghton Mifflin, 2006.

SmartGirl.org. "Latest Survey Results: Report on Teen Read Week 2005." http://www.smartgirl.org/reports/5100284.html.

Stanovich, K. E., and A. E. Cunningham. "Studying the Consequences of Literacy within a Literate Society: The Cognitive Correlates of Print Exposure." *Memory and Cognition* 20 (1992): 51–68.

Starr, Carol. "A Brief History of the Young Adult Services Division." *Young Adult Library Services Association Handbook*. http://www.ala.org/ala/yalsa/aboutyalsa/briefhistory.htm.

Swets, Paul W. *The Art of Talking With Your Teenager*. Holbrook, MA: Adams Media Corporation, 1995.

Trott, Barry. "Looking for a Good Book? Developing an Online Readers' Advisory Suggestion Service." Program, National Public Library Association Conference, Boston, MA, March 23, 2006.

Ujiie, Joanne, and Stephen Krashen. "Home Run Books and Reading Enjoyment." *Knowledge Quest* 31, no. 1 (2002): 36–37.

Walsh, David. *Why Do They Act That Way?* New York: Free Press, 2004.

Wyatt, Neal. *The Readers' Advisory Guide to Nonfiction*. Chicago: ALA Editions, 2007.

Index

Heather Booth specializes in young adult services in the Readers' Advisory and Audio Services Department at the Downers Grove Public Library in Illinois. In addition to selecting materials and coordinating services for the library's Teen Central, she serves as a coordinator for the library's long-standing teen advisory board, which was honored as a nominating group for YALSA's Teens' Top Ten award for the 2005 and 2006 seasons. She earned a BA in English Literature from Kalamazoo College in Kalamazoo, Michigan, and an MS from the University of Illinois Graduate School of Library and Information Sciences in Champaign. Her lifelong love of books and reading led her to librarianship, and she chose to specialize in public library teen services out of a desire to serve the dynamic needs and interests of young people in a community-based setting. In 2002 she was initiated into Beta Phi Mu, the International Honor Society for Library and Information Science.